Hockey Is Our Game

HOCKEY IS OUR GAME 🍁

Jim Coleman

Canada in the World of International Hockey

KEY PORTER·BOOKS

Canadian Cataloguing in Publication Data

Coleman, Jim
    Hockey is our game
ISBN 1-55013-056-0

1. Hockey - Canada - History.   2. Hockey Canada.
I. Title.
GV848.4.C3C64 1987   796.96'26   C87-094691-9

Design Catherine Wilson for C.P. Wilson Graphic Communication
Typesetting Imprint Typesetting
Printed and bound in Canada by D.W. Friesen and Sons

Key Porter Books Limited
70 The Esplanade
Toronto, Ontario
Canada M5E 1R2

87 88 89 90   6 5 4 3 2 1

CONTENTS

Acknowledgments

THIS PROJECT WAS INITIATED AND SUPPORTED BY THE DIRECTORS of Hockey Canada, who felt that the time had come for someone to publish a book recording the activities of their organization since it was chartered by the federal government in 1969.

The Directors acceded readily to my suggestion that the history of Hockey Canada should provide the foundation for a slightly more ambitious history of Canada's involvement in international hockey since 1920. The indulgence of the Directors has permitted me to write a personal narrative, in which I have attempted to record how international tournaments impinged upon the consciousness of one Canadian who has been a lifelong devotee of The Game.

There will be readers who take issue with my interpretation of international events. To them, I stress the fact that I do not profess to be a scholarly historian. The opinions expressed here reflect many personal prejudices.

There are many individuals who have assisted in the preparation of this manuscript. The list begins with Christopher Lang and the entire staff of Hockey Canada in Toronto and Calgary.

I am indebted to the officers of Pacific Press, Ltd., including E.H. "Bill" Wheatley, Norman Weitzel and George Hutchison, who generously provided me with working accommodations. Two women at Pacific Press, Paula Ingles and Annette Buddin, were most helpful. And, I received the complete cooperation of the library staff of the *Vancouver Sun* and the *Vancouver Province*.

Many others, including old newspaper and hockey friends, assisted me. I acknowledge, gratefully, the help of Father David Bauer, Jack Sullivan, David King, Vincent Leah, Harry Sinden, John Ferguson, Hal Sigurdson, Jim Kearney, Denny Boyd, Bob Dunn, Maggie Coleman, Milton Dunnell, George Gross, Duncan Stewart, Archie McDonald, Kent Gilchrist, William Hay, Douglas Fisher, Don Fleming, Terry O'Malley and Rick Noonan. I apologize to any whose names inadvertently have been omitted.

Foreword

Any mention of Team Canada and international hockey brings into perfect focus the 1972 series between Canada and the Soviet Union. Paul Henderson's climactic goal was watched by almost every Canadian, and our pride in our country swelled to amazing heights. September 28, 1972, was the most outstanding day in history for Canadian sports. That incredible series is just part of the mosaic of Canada's participation in international hockey.

Jim Coleman has been involved with almost every important international hockey event in the last 50 years. His personal contribution to successes Canadian teams have enjoyed should not go unmentioned. As chief negotiator for Canada since 1974, I have been able to rely on Jim's judgment and advice to our international program's benefit.

Hockey Is Our Game is not only the history of international hockey. It also provides an insight into the negotiations and events that have meant so much to Canadian hockey fans in all parts of the world.

R. Alan Eagleson

Victor Kuzkin salutes a victorious Peter Mahovlich. Brian Pickell

THE WINNING GOAL, MOSCOW, 1972

ALMOST ANY ADULT CANADIAN CAN TELL YOU EXACTLY WHAT HE or she was doing on September 28, 1972, when Paul Henderson scored the 6-5 goal at 19:26 of the final period. It was nighttime in Moscow, but was still morning or early afternoon in most parts of Canada. For a tenth of a second, our world stood still. Then, as the red light flickered behind Vladislav Tretiak, our hearts exploded with joy.

A visitor from Mars could have been forgiven for asking, "Why all this hysteria? It's only a hockey game!"

You are only half-right, Spaceman. It *was* only a hockey game. But it was a hockey game of a lifetime. It was a game that gave all Canadians an overwhelming sense of national vindication. For the first time, our best professionals had played an eight-game series against the Soviets. And our players had beaten them!

Mind you, it was a near-run thing. If Henderson hadn't shoved that rebounding puck under Tretiak at 19:26 of the third period in that particular game, the famous Summit Series of 1972 would have ended in a draw — three wins and two ties for each team. And the Soviets would have claimed victory because they outscored Canada, 27 goals to 26, over the first seven games.

Henderson's winning goal was, for me, the culmination of more than half a century of feverish, unabashedly chauvinistic hockey-viewing.

It had been one hell of a long way from Winnipeg to downtown Moscow. I had seen Canada's first world championship hockey team — the Winnipeg Falcons, who won the Olympic Games at Antwerp in 1920 — and, now, in September, 1972, I had remained on the scene long enough to see Canada re-establish its hockey dominance after 20 frustrating years of bitterly disappointing defeats.

Going into the 1988 Winter Olympics at Calgary, Canada hasn't won an Olympic title since the Edmonton Mercurys triumphed at Oslo in 1952. Even more humiliating is our record in those annual tournaments that the Europeans of the International Ice Hockey Federation have been pleased to advertise as the "world championships." Our pride had been damaged, almost irreparably, when the Soviets whipped the Toronto Lyndhursts 7-2, at Stockholm in 1954. Thereafter, Canada regained a modicum of respectability when the Penticton Vees won the 1955 world tournament in West Germany in 1955. The Whitby Dunlops won at Oslo in 1958; the Belleville McFarlands won at Prague in 1959; and the Trail Smoke-Eaters won at Geneva in 1961.

But since the Trail Smoke-Eaters of 1961, we had been blanked. The good Lord alone knows what would have happened to our national morale if Paul Henderson hadn't popped that goal in the Luzhniki Ice Palace on the night of September 28.

In some respects, Paul Henderson was an unlikely candidate for immortality. He had scored 38 goals for the Toronto Maple Leafs in a 78-game schedule the previous season. Although he was a brilliantly speedy skater, he was something of an oddity: a right-handed shot playing left wing. Years earlier, Lester Patrick, coach of the New York Rangers, had experimented successfully by playing left-handed shots on right wing. Two of those transplanted lefties — Cecil Dillon and Bryan Hextall — won the NHL scoring championship. But, in 1972, you didn't see too many right-handers playing left wing in the NHL.

There were other peculiarities in Henderson's job profile. Throughout his career, he had suffered from asthma and was bothered by the cold temperatures at ice-level. At one stage, the Detroit Red Wings had him wearing a mask when he was on the ice.

Henderson also was one of the first NHL players to don a helmet. He wore it continuously on the ice after suffering a concussion from a headfirst crash into the boards at Maple Leaf Gardens. It took courage to wear a helmet in the NHL in the 1970s. Headgear was disdained by most players, who regarded it as cumbersome and unnecessary. *All* the Soviet players wore helmets. They had been wearing them since their first appearance in international hockey in 1954. The Soviets weren't idiots — they believed in protecting their brains.

In short: there was little in Paul Henderson's previous record to suggest that he was going to be the individual scoring star of the greatest hockey series ever to be staged.

Henderson was prominent in the first four matches on Canadian ice; he

John Ferguson, Team Canada's assistant coach. *Brian Pickell*

Yvan Cournoyer ties the score at 5-5. *Brian Pickell*

scored in Game One at Montreal and he scored again in Game Three at Winnipeg. But, later, it became evident that he had been gearing up for the greatest performance of his lifetime.

Possibly it was the brisk Moscow September air that gave him an added shot of jet propulsion when the series shifted to the Soviet Union. In any event, he scored what *should* have been the winning goal in Game Five; he scored the winning goal in Game Six and the winning goal in Game Seven. All these leading up to his never-to-be-forgotten goal in Game Eight.

As if it were only yesterday, I remember exactly what I was doing at 19:26 of that third period. I was sitting in Luzhniki Ice Palace, but I was about as far away as you could be from the net into which Henderson made his winning shot. There was no North American-type press box for the visiting media. We sat among the spectators about 12 rows up from the ice-surface and midway between the blueline and the net at the other end of the arena.

At approximately 17:00 of the second period, I had left my seat in a sweaty fit of frustration. The Soviets had just scored two successive goals to take a 5-3 lead. The Canadians were working their butts off; however, it appeared to be a doomed enterprise.

I left because I was unreasonably angry. My reaction was childish. My unworthy thoughts went something like this: "Why the hell did we have to come all the way to Moscow to be humiliated by these Russkies? Why didn't we stay home and mind our own business?"

I walked up two flights of stairs to the media bar. Although I had many years of sobriety on my blotter at that point, I toyed seriously with the thought of ordering a double vodka. I sat there through the intermission after the second period and failed to return to rinkside for the start of the third period. It was shameful; the Canadians were out on the ice, giving the grittiest performance of their lives, and I was sulking in the media bar.

For possibly half an hour I stayed there, but I didn't order that double vodka. In the distance, I could hear the roars of the crowd after the final period began. Then, early in the period, there was a strange hush. Someone came into the room and announced that Phil Esposito had scored for Canada, reducing the Soviet margin to 5-4. I quickly decided that there was a good luck charm connected with my seat in the bar. I would stay there until the game was finished.

While I was listening to the ebb and flow of the crowd noises in the distance, Trent Frayne rushed into the bar. He and I had been sitting in adjoining seats in the media area. Frayne burbled happily: "You've got to come and see this! Mad Dog Gilbert just got into a fight. He and a Russkie are serving major penalties."

Rod Gilbert, a genteel right-winger from the New York Rangers, had been a model of decorum throughout the previous three games. Quite unfairly, Frayne and I had nicknamed him "Mad Dog" for the purposes of our private conversations.

Something big was happening if Gilbert had been impelled to lose his temper and turn to fisticuffing. Obviously, the fires of optimism still must be burning brightly in the breast of every member of Team Canada. Suddenly, hope was restored in my own craven heart. Frayne led me, babbling, back to our seats, where we watched the remaining 15 minutes of the game — a quarter hour of sheer insanity.

Across the way from the media seats — but in the same end of the arena — our 2,700 North American rooters were waving Canadian flags and maintaining a continuous clamour. Even after three previous nights of exposure to this Canadian brand of hyper-enthusiasm, the Russian spectators were awed. I don't blame them. I've never heard hockey fans make as much noise as those 2,700 created in the Luzhniki Ice Palace.

The Soviets are quick learners, though. They realized that they had made a serious mistake in seating all the Canadian supporters in the same section of the rink. It was obvious that the continuous cheering from their fans was providing the Team Canada players with a great deal of emotional stimulus.

Team Canada coach Harry Sinden. *Brian Pickell*

The 2,700 North Americans were making more noise than the 10,000 Russians in the other sections of the building.

So, for crucial Game Eight, the Soviets created their own "cheering section" of 500 voices and seated them right smack-dab next to the Canadians. This cheering section was well rehearsed. They waved Soviet flags, and their chants of "shy-boom, shy-boom" countered every outburst of Canadian cheering. However, as the wild tempo of period three in Game Eight reached a crescendo, it was apparent that the Soviet cheering section was badly overmatched.

Let it be remembered that the introduction of the "cheering section" was only one more manifestation of the Russians' willingness to go to almost any lengths to win. Much more importantly, they had forced Team Canada to accept two myopic referees, Josef Kompalla and Rudy Bata, to officiate in the final game.

Right from the start, there was a feeling that all hell was likely to break loose. In the first period, Kompalla called an interference penalty on Jean-Paul Parise. Outraged, Parise banged his stick on the ice. Kompalla promptly added a ten-minute misconduct penalty.

Now, Parise had never received a misconduct penalty in his five years of NHL competition. So, maddened beyond reason, he raised his stick over his head and appeared ready to decapitate Kompalla with a two-hander. The ashen-faced referee skated rapidly to the penalty box, whereupon the bilingual announcer told the crowd that Parise would be thrown out of the game.

The Canadians in the Ice Palace blew their stacks. While they were chanting "Let's Go Home! Let's Go Home!", Harry Sinden, the Canadian coach, threw a stool on the ice. The stool shattered. Intent on delaying the game as long as possible, Sinden picked up John Ferguson's chair and hurled it onto the ice, too. Ferguson, Sinden's assistant coach, joined the fray by screaming until his eyes bulged.

Although it was a riotous evening, the two teams were playing magnificent hockey. When Frayne led me back to my seat, we were in plenty of time to join in the incredibly loud outburst of Canadian braying as Yvan Cournoyer tied the score at 5-5 with a spectacular goal at 12:56.

More turmoil! When Cournoyer shot the puck into the net, the goal-judge failed to flash the red light. He alibied later that the electric switch malfunctioned but his word was suspect. He was Viktor Dombrovski, an off-duty Soviet referee who was to become Canada's *bête noire* in future international matches.

This new outrage had us going bananas. Most of us in the Canadian news media section had seen Cournoyer raise his stick to signal "goal." We were totally confused when the red light didn't flash behind the net.

Thereupon ensued one of the craziest scenes in the history of international sports. Alan Eagleson leaped from his box seat on the opposite side of the arena, directly across from where the team benches were situated. The executive director of the NHL Players' Association explained later that he was intent on rushing to the end of the rink to remonstrate with the goal-judge.

Whatever his intentions, Eagleson's vault over the box railing was grossly misinterpreted by the uniformed militiamen who ringed the arena at ice-level. (They had been stationed there since the Canadian players erupted after Parise's match penalty in the first ten minutes of the game.) Eagleson's leap deposited him right on the shoulders of the militiamen and, thoroughly startled, half a dozen of them seized him. They were far from gentle in their efforts to restrain him. Eagleson began to bellow for assistance as he struggled with his captors.

Out on the ice, the Canadian players quickly became aware of Eagleson's plight. With towering Peter Mahovlich in the van, they swarmed across the ice, their sticks raised menacingly. Mahovlich led the charge over the boards, and the militiamen pulled back in confusion.

It was a bizarre performance. The players hauled Eagleson over the boards and onto the ice. His spectacles had been partially dislodged in the scuffle and were dangling from one ear as the players half-dragged, half-carried him across the rink to the Canadian bench. Midway across the ice, Eagleson jabbed the middle finger of one hand in the air in an unmistakably rude gesture of defiance.

The Soviet spectators, trained from infancy to respect uniformed authority, sat in bewildered silence. They didn't even bother to whistle, which is their form of booing. They were just plain damned puzzled by the show.

Many televiewers throughout the western world may have shared the Russian bewilderment. Some Canadians, back in their homes where they were insulated from the blazing emotions of the moment, later sat down to write indignant letters to their local newspapers. Eagleson, they said, had besmirched the name of our country with his ridiculous re-enactment of Eliza Crossing the Ice.

Looking back on it, I'm convinced that the Soviet hockey players were "spooked" by the extra-curricular craziness. They appeared to be awe-struck by all the undisciplined flouting of authority. In any event, the Soviets suddenly and uncharacteristically went into their shells. Possibly their brain-trusters had told them that if Game Eight ended in a 5-5 tie, they were going to claim a series victory because they had outscored the Canadians, 32 goals to 31.

In fact, the Soviets had lost the initiative about two minutes before Cournoyer scored. After Eagleson's ice-dance and the Canadian assault on the Moscow militia, they never regained the offensive free-wheeling which had been the secret of their success throughout the first seven games and fifty minutes of the series.

But, oh, it still was magnificent end-to-end hockey. Most of us in the Canadian media section were muttering that the tide had turned — the Russians might not score another goal. Indeed, some of us had resigned ourselves to the possibility that *neither* team would score. For many of us, after the gut-wrenching ups-and-downs of that incredible evening, a tied series might have been acceptable.

The members of Team Canada, on the other hand, weren't ready to settle for a tied series. Nothing less than a clear-cut win would satisfy the Canadian hockey players. In the dressing room after the second period, Sinden had told them to play carefully in the first ten minutes after the intermission, concentrating chiefly on preventing any further Soviet scoring. Then, said Sinden, turn on your after-burners for the final ten minutes — gamble for goals!

The Esposito goal at 2:27 of that third period was an unexpected benison. Perhaps the Soviets began to have some misgivings at that point. Looking back on it, it's probable that they were beginning to switch to the defensive even before little Cournoyer scored his game deadlocker.

With less than one minute remaining, Sinden decided to make a line change. Dennis Hull, who was playing on Jean Ratelle's line, skated over to Sinden and said, "Harry, you don't really want me out here at a time like this." Sinden agreed and decided to go with the line of Bobby Clarke, Henderson and Ron

Ellis. But, fortunately for Canada's hockey history, Esposito refused to come to the bench for the final minute.

The action was so intense in those final seconds that it is necessary to re-examine slow-motion pictures of the climax.

Henderson comes down left wing at full throttle. He shoots from the near-rim of the face-off circle, and Tretiak makes the stop. But the goalie lets the rebound get away from him.

Henderson is skating so swiftly that he falls as he reaches the corner of the net. He crashes into the backboards. Instinctively, he leaps to his skates and comes out from behind the net, less than six feet from Tretiak's crease.

Meanwhile, after Henderson's initial shot, the puck has rebounded towards *three* Soviet players. Inexplicably, none of the Soviets is able to control the puck and it slides to Esposito, who has crossed through the Soviet defence zone from right wing to left wing.

Esposito shoots while *four* Soviet players are lunging at him. None of the four comes close enough to interfere with his shot. Tretiak stops Esposito's hard shot, but the goalie is unable to smother the rebound.

Having regained his feet, Henderson has rushed out from behind the net. He is almost close enough to be touched by Tretiak's right hand. Crossing the net from left to right, Henderson picks up Esposito's rebound and shoots at point-blank range.

Again, Tretiak gives up a rebound. And Henderson, still in full flight across the goal-mouth from left to right, jams the puck behind Tretiak, who is sprawled in the crease.

GOAL! The puck hits the back of the net, about six inches above ice-level. Henderson really puts his heart into that final shot. This time goal-judge Viktor Dombrovski flashes the red light!

You may have been 5,000 miles from Luzhniki Ice Palace — back home in North America — but your view of the winning goal was infinitely superior to the media's view in the arena. We were approximately 150 feet from the spot where Henderson fired three shots at Tretiak in a time-frame that was not much longer than three snaps of your fingers. What we did see was Henderson raising his stick in triumph. We saw the red light flashing at the far end of the arena. We saw Henderson being mobbed by the entire contingent of Canadian players, howling ecstatically.

Before I recovered from my delirium, I was standing on my seat, acting like an imbecile. There I was, a 62-year-old man, clad in my sincere-blue three-piece suit, my old school tie and my pin-collar shirt. (Don Cherry and I are the only hockey observers who insist on wearing old-fashioned pin-collar shirts.) There I was, turning around to face Leonid Brezhnev and the other Soviet Politburo members in their back-row seats, and jamming my clenched right fist and arm upwards in repeated gestures, which were obviously never intended to be interpreted as "Aloha."

My parents, who brought me up properly, would have been ashamed of me. But I felt no shame — only exultation! I was gloating in the realization that I was present for the most significant victory in the history of Canadian sports.

Jubilant Canadian fans in the Luzhniki Ice Palace.
Brian Pickell

Most of my Canadian media-mates were similarly demented. A Swiss newspaperman, sitting two rows below us, was staring up at our antics with a puzzled half-smile on his face, muttering, "Animals! Animals!"

The remaining 34 seconds of the game were only a happy blur. Sinden called his players to the bench before the post-goal face-off. He told them simply to dump the puck into the Soviet end at every opportunity. The Soviets never came over their own blueline. As the siren sounded, Sinden, Ferguson, Eagleson and a dozen other Canadians skidded across the ice to join the players in an orgy of mutual congratulations.

It is worth mentioning the Moscow hockey crowd at this point. Although crestfallen, they were punctilious in their observance of the niceties. I can still see them, standing there somberly while the two teams lined up at their

respective bluelines and the Canadian flag was slowly raised to the roof (appropriately, at the same end of the arena where Henderson had scored). As "O Canada" was played on the public-address system, the music was drowned out by the singing of 2,700 Canadians. Only in wartime could you have heard our national anthem bellowed with such unbridled emotion.

Ten seconds after the last notes sounded in the arena, I glanced across at the seats that had been occupied by the Soviet special corps of 500 rooters. They had been there while the anthem was being played, but, in the next ten seconds, the seats had emptied — just as if a trapdoor had opened to drop the 500 into the basement.

The manner in which the hockey players celebrated the victory was their own business. While the players were celebrating, the wretches of the press were sitting in front of their portable typewriters, pounding out thousands of words of breathless prose.

I know that no one slept more than a few fitful winks that night. We had to get up at 4 A.M. to catch an Aeroflot flight to Prague, Czechoslovakia, on the first leg of our trip home to Canada. It was still dark when the team bus and the media bus left the Intourist Hotel for the Moscow Airport.

The media bus reeked of stale vodka. Raisa, who had acted as the media interpreter for the past nine days, occupied, as usual, the jump-seat right next to the bus driver. She made no comment on the previous night's hockey game. Her stiff-upper-lip demeanour suggested that she would be relieved to see us leave the country.

While we were sitting in the airport departure lounge, buying scalding coffee and postcards to get rid of our few remaining rubles, a familiar figure appeared. It was Usevolod Bobrov, the senior coach of the defeated Soviet hockey team. He was heading for the gate from which a domestic flight was leaving and was accompanied by two men who, like himself, appeared to be Army types.

A hung-over Canadian newspaperman suggested that Bobrov was on his way to exile in Siberia. Bobrov had his greatcoat draped from his shoulders in the approved European fashion. He was smoking a cigarette. The hung-over wag couldn't resist the opportunity to suggest that it was his *last* cigarette before he faced the firing squad.

The relatively brief flight from Moscow to Prague was quite ghastly. Reminiscent of the press bus, the Soviet airplane — at least our section of it — reeked of hangovers and stale vodka.

As we broke through the heavy overcast and the pilot swung us into line with the runway lights at Prague Airport, a wonderfully warm feeling chased all doubts about the series from my troubled mind. With all its rowdy imperfections, the hockey of the past 27 days had reached an unexcelled level of competition. For sheer sustained emotion, nothing, in my experience, ever matched it.

Game Eight, in Moscow on September 28, 1972, was the most memorable event in the lifetime of any Canadian hockey enthusiast. And I had been there. As the plane landed, I felt a surge of gratitude that I would always remember this as the absolute peak of excitement and satisfaction in more than 40 years of involvement in sports. And I accepted the fact that, even if I lived to be 100, never again would I see anything to equal it.

The famous picture of Paul Henderson after his goal of a lifetime. *The Toronto Star*
Soviet coaches Usevolod Bobrov (left) and Boris Kulagin (right) with Andrei Starevoitov, General Secretary of the Soviet Ice Hockey Federation. *Brian Pickell*

Georges Vézina, the Montreal Canadiens' star goalie from 1910 to 1926.
Hockey Hall of Fame

2 THE MAKINGS OF A HOCKEY FAN

THE TRAIL THAT LED ME TO MOSCOW IN 1972 BEGAN IN WINNIPEG in 1920. As a young boy I heard our sardonic elders describe the Manitoba climate as "nine months of winter and three months of poor skating weather." This was an inside joke, exclusively for local consumption. Any out-of-town visitor who disparaged our climate was asking for a mouthful of knuckles.

It wasn't all that bad, really. We had langorously hot summers with occasional thunderstorms of such shattering violence that they scared the hell out of a small boy. We had autumns that were unequalled for their kaleidoscopic splendour. And, without question, on most evenings, Winnipeg enjoyed the most beautiful sunsets this side of paradise.

Winnipeg was hockey heartland. In that context, it was appropriate that the first Canadian team ever to win an Olympic hockey championship came from Winnipeg.

The Winnipeg Falcons, composed almost exclusively of Manitoba-born Icelanders, went to Antwerp, Belgium, in 1920 for the first Winter Olympics to include ice hockey. The only non-Icelander on Canada's winning team was Huck Woodman, who was of British stock although his name certainly sounded Icelandic. Woodman meshed nicely with his Icelandic teammates whose names were Fredrickson, Johanneson, Haldarson, Fridfinnson, Goodman, Benson and Byron.

Every male child in Winnipeg played hockey in some form. The kids whose families couldn't afford to buy skates, played shinny in the streets with frozen road-apples, contributed gratuitously by the horses which pulled the delivery sleighs for the milk company, the bread company and other merchants.

Winnipeg schoolboys of that era wore animal-hide moccasins or shoe-packs throughout the winter. No one who grew up in Winnipeg in the 1920s will ever forget the darkly pungent odour produced by 40 or 50 pairs of wet moccasins in a classroom. One whiff of those wet moccasins would clear your sinuses — permanently!

Our home was at 52 Donald Street, only half a block north of the Assiniboine River. In 1920, this was still comparatively deluxe residential property. Directly north of us lived Hugh Paterson whose son, Senator Norman M. Paterson, became one of Canada's wealthiest grain merchants and shipowners. In the next house south of us lived Captain Spink, one of whose grandchildren, Richard Bowles, became Lieutenant-Governor of Manitoba.

My mother taught me to skate, indoors, at the old Winnipeg Rink, which was a few doors north of Portage Avenue on Langside Street. In 1920, the rink was owned by W.J. Holmes. The Winnipeg Skating Club was one of Mr. Holmes's rental tenants. My mother was an excellent figure-skater and, for my initial flight on ice, she gave me a kitchen chair and told me to shove it in front of me.

Her fellow-members of the Winnipeg Skating Club were much too polite to curse me, but I was aware of some extremely baleful glances as I steered my chair into those restricted areas where competent figure-skaters were cutting their figure-eights or warming up for their Axel Paulsens. Even now, I can recall that the club professional, a Mr. Anderson, bared his teeth rather wolfishly when my chair nudged him in the buttocks.

At that juncture, my mother withdrew me from public exhibition. She told me to sit in the club-room at the south end of the rink while she had her practice session under Mr. Anderson's supervision. I sat there, sulking, until she came off the ice. My mother, who always was a blithe spirit, mollified her brooding infant by taking me to Dell's Ice Cream Parlor and buying me a banana cone. It was winter, admittedly, but Dell's ice cream was so delectable that it knew no season.

To save her fellow-members of the Winnipeg Skating Club from any further distress, my mother bought me a pair of Automobile-D Skates and directed me to conduct any further skating experiments in the Great Outdoors. Accordingly, I betook myself to what was known then as "The River Rinks." This was a public recreational area on the frozen Assiniboine River at the foot of Kennedy Street. It was only slightly more than four blocks from our house on Donald.

As I turned the corner of Donald onto Assiniboine Avenue, confronting me was the residence of Madame Gauthier. Now, this was a semi-shrine for Winnipeg sports fans. I don't know what position Monsieur Gauthier occupied in the Winnipeg Establishment, but Madame Gauthier was a celebrity — her brother was Tony Gingras!

You've never heard of Tony Gingras? Well, Tony was a distinguished member of the Winnipeg Victorias, the first team to win the Stanley Cup. Yes, that's correct — the Winnipeg Victorias won the Stanley Cup in January, 1891, the very first year it was offered for competition for the hockey championship of Canada.

Tony Gingras played on the 1891 team with Dan Bain and the Flett brothers, Rod and Magnus. They went to Montreal and defeated the Montreal Sham-rocks, two-straight, in a proposed two-out-of-three game series. On January 29, the Victorias won, 4-3, and two nights later they won again, 2-1, after four minutes of overtime. Merely passing the home of Tony Gingras's sister every afternoon made me feel like a hockey player, even if I was fated to spend my life on the sidelines as an observer.

The River Rinks were the mecca for all aspiring young athletes in the south-central section of Winnipeg. This was strictly open-air stuff; there was no protection from the elements when the temperature dropped to 30 below zero. There was a large area for pleasure-skating; a boarded area for hockey shinny; and a large structure — a toboggan slide — which was erected each winter on the river ice at the western end of the complex. Actually, there was one bit of shelter — a long wooden building where you changed into your skates. If you were big enough and strong enough, you could find a place in front of the pot-bellied stoves to thaw your frozen feet.

On countless late afternoons, I walked home along the Assiniboine River under the blinking street lamps, tears freezing on my cheeks as my semi-thawed feet struck the bumps of frozen snow on the sidewalks. Ask any old Winnipegger — most men over 70 in that city still walk with a limp because they froze their toes so frequently on the River Rinks. My mother, who believed in Spartan measures for the wounded, would make me sit on the front verandah while she rubbed my feet with snow.

From the very outset, I was overmatched on the Rinks. Although I had good skates and good hockey equipment, I, quite simply, didn't have the skating ability or the skills of 95 percent of the kids who skimmed over the frozen river. I couldn't carry the puck the length of my pointed little nose, my eye-glasses were an encumbrance, and most of the time I ended up skating around fruitlessly.

Years later, my friend, Himie Koshevoy, a Vancouver sports editor, was writing about the performance of Lude Palm, a winger for Guy Patrick's Vancouver Lions, in a game against the Portland Buckaroos. He wrote, "Lude Palm pursued the puck valiantly all night — but, never was he able to catch up with it." Himie could have been describing my futile efforts to compete on the River Rinks.

I couldn't play the damn game. My plight was complicated by the fact that, between the ages of ten and eighteen, I spent my time in a maximum security boarding school in Victoria, and we didn't have any ice on which to skate. However, the victory of the Winnipeg Falcons at the 1920 Olympics gave me a lifelong addiction to the sport of hockey — even if it was only as a press box spectator.

It was my father, D.C. Coleman, who was responsible for my addiction. He was the most well-read sports enthusiast I've ever known, and hockey was his lifelong love. Later, he would become chairman and president of Canadian Pacific's farflung transportation and business enterprises, but the position that brought him his greatest personal pleasure was his vice-presidency of the Canadian Arena Company. In that capacity, he was also vice-president of the Montreal Canadiens hockey club for the final 22 years of his life.

My father encouraged my interest in hockey by providing me with the opportunity to see the best. For instance, at the age of ten, he sent me alone on the train (in the care of the sleeping-car conductor) to Regina. There my father's friend, A.E. Whitmore, took me to see the Vancouver Maroons defeat the Regina Capitals for the right to travel east and play the Toronto St. Pat's in the 1922 Stanley Cup final.

When I was attending University School, my boarding school in Victoria, my father made it possible for me to see three games of the 1925 Stanley Cup finals when the Victoria Cougars defeated the Montreal Canadiens. He arranged for H.G. Wilson, manager of the Empress Hotel, to introduce me to Howie Morenz, Georges Vézina and "Odie" Cleghorn, three of the Canadiens who were staying at the hotel.

Back at school, I was careful to refrain from telling any of the other inmates that I had met three of the world's greatest hockey players. They would have cuffed me into silence and dismissed me as a pretentious little jerk. It was wise to keep some things to yourself.

Two years after Victoria won the Stanley Cup by defeating Montreal, the Canadian Amateur Hockey Association awarded the Allan Cup finals to the City of Vancouver. The finalists for the Canadian championship were the University of Toronto Grads and Fort William. Pulling some strings with the school authorities, my father arranged for me to go to Vancouver for the games. I was ensconced in solitary splendour in a room of my own in the old Hotel Vancouver on the corner of Granville and Georgia streets. My father had obtained a pair of tickets for the series. One of the hotel porters took me to each game and supervised my nightly return to the hotel.

You'll gather that my father was, where his children were concerned, a very thoughtful man. In that context, it wasn't difficult to persuade him to take me to see the Winnipeg Falcons after their Olympic triumph. The exploits of the Falcons were a common dinner-table topic in our house in 1920. A frequent

The Winnipeg Falcons, 1920.
Hockey Hall of Fame

participant in the discussions was Hugh Baird, a broker who operated a seat on the Winnipeg Grain Exchange for James Norris, the same James Norris who afterwards controlled the Chicago Stadium and the Detroit Red Wings. Hugh Baird had played hockey for the Montreal Amateur Hockey Association in the days when the Stanley Cup was a trophy for amateur teams. After moving from his native Montreal to Winnipeg, he acted as a referee in several Stanley Cup playoffs.

The Falcons returned home to a tumultuous civic welcome in April, 1920. Because there was no artificial ice in the Winnipeg Amphitheatre, their fellow-Winnipeggers had to wait until the following December to see their heroes compete in their first post-Olympics exhibition. All summer long, I had been badgering my father and Mr. Baird to take me to that first game, which would be played against a Winnipeg All-Star Team. They didn't fail me.

It was the first time that I had seen a hockey game in an enclosed arena. Accordingly, my first sight of the Winnipeg Falcons was a dazzling experience. The Winnipeg Amphitheatre on Whitehall Street wasn't more than a mile from our Donald Street home. It was operated by W.J. Holmes, the same man who operated the Winnipeg Rink where I had learned to skate. Although the building seated only 5,000 spectators, to my childish eyes, it was an immense bowl of blazing lights, excited humanity and continual noise.

Almost 70 years later, I'd like to be able to tell you that I remember every detail of my first indoor hockey match. The truth is that I was so dazzled by the spectacle that I can recall only those magnificent Icelanders, none of the All-Stars who played against them. To the delight of their admirers, the Falcons won, but the score eludes me.

One player, Mike Goodman, held me spellbound. Goodman was a champion speed-skater as well as being a superb hockey player. Even now, I have a vivid recollection of Mike pirouetting on his blades and skating *backwards* as he checked the incoming forwards of the opposing team.

Sitting between my father and Mr. Baird in their heavy raccoon coats, which were *de rigeur* wintertime wear in Winnipeg, I was hooked, inextricably. I would be a hockey fan for the remainder of my life.

It is necessary to understand that, in the third decade of this century, hockey was *the* game in Western Canada. There was baseball, some soccer and Canadian rugby-football was a brief autumnal pastime, but hockey was the consuming passion of every small boy growing up on the Prairies.

An eight-year-old Winnipeg boy lived in a very small world. As far as Winnipeggers were concerned, the two major sporting events of the entire year were the Allan Cup finals and the Memorial Cup finals. The Allan Cup was emblematic of the senior amateur hockey championship of Canada. The Memorial Cup was a new trophy for the junior hockey championship of Canada. There was no professional hockey in Winnipeg until the mid-1920s when Billy Holmes's team, the Maroons, played for a few seasons in a minor league, the American Association.

In our tiny world, we believed passionately that hockey was exclusively a Canadian sport. It was heresy to suggest that the game could be played expertly by the citizens of any other country. Those of us who were old enough to read the reports of the 1920 Olympics in the three local newspapers — the

Winnipeg Tribune, the *Telegram* or the morning paper, which was known then as the *Manitoba Free Press* — were astounded to learn that the Americans, too, played hockey.

In the tournament at Antwerp, the Falcons overwhelmed Czechoslovakia, 15-0, and they whipped Sweden, 12-1. But the Americans gave the Canadians a very interesting test before being beaten, 2-0. There was no reason why we should have been surprised — the northern sections of the United States, particularly the Midwest and New England, shared the generally glacial winter climate of Canada.

In those days, no one ever dreamed that the Soviet Union would become a hockey power. It was just beginning to emerge from the blood-stained ruins of the Russian Empire, and three more decades would pass before the Soviets would perfect their own brand of ice hockey. To our national consternation, their brand proved to be a brilliant athletic art form.

Of course, the Americans had some early input into Canadian hockey, even in ultra-chauvinistic Winnipeg. Many young Canadian hockey players owed their survival to that revered American weekly magazine, *The Saturday Evening Post.*

A large percentage of Prairie parents couldn't afford to buy manufactured shin-pads for their hockey-playing moppets. The *Post* was an admirable substitute. It was much taller, in format, than other magazines. Placed inside a hockey stocking, it provided excellent protection from skate-top to knee.

In Winnipeg, hockey players were everyone's childhood heroes. With no professional hockey in their own city, young Winnipeggers took vicarious pleasure in the performance of local players who had gone on to perform in the professional ranks.

Professional hockey was played in two widely separated sections of Canada. The National Hockey League operated in Eastern Canada with teams in Montreal, Toronto, Ottawa, Quebec and, later, Hamilton. Out on the Pacific Coast, Frank Patrick and Lester Patrick ran their own league with teams in Vancouver, Victoria and — of all places — Seattle! Closer to home, the Western Canada League was about to emerge as a full-fledged professional group with teams in Calgary, Edmonton, Saskatoon and Regina.

Back in Winnipeg, we could look around those leagues and see an abundance of heroes from Manitoba. Two of those great Winnipeg Falcons, Frank Fredrickson and "Slim" Haldarson, went to play for the Victoria Cougars. After the Cougars disbanded in 1926, they went to Detroit in the NHL. Fredrickson continued to be one of the great stars of the National Hockey League with the Boston Bruins. Bobby Benson, the tiny Falcon defenceman, played for several teams in the Western Canada League and then, like Fredrickson, joined the Boston Bruins when they were admitted to the NHL. It intrigued me to see that my favourite Falcon, Mike Goodman, never made the NHL. He played minor league professional hockey for many years before retiring to Florida, where he outlived all his teammates from the 1920 Olympic championship.

By 1921, two other Winnipeg graduates, Red Dutton and Harry Oliver, were playing for the Calgary Tigers. They went to a Stanley Cup final with Calgary in 1924. After the Western Canada League disbanded, Oliver played for Boston and Dutton went to the Montreal Maroons. Dutton became the playing-coach and manager of the New York Americans and, later still, he became president of the National Hockey League.

In the Western Canada League, the Edmonton Eskimos had two stalwarts from our neighbouring town of Selkirk: "Bullet-Joe" Simpson and "Crutchy" Morrison. Both had played amateur hockey for the Selkirk Fishermen in the Winnipeg and District Senior Amateur League.

The Regina Capitals had almost a full roster of former Winnipeggers. Their forward line was composed of Dick Irvin, George Hay and Emory "Spunk" Sparrow. One of their heavy-hitting defencemen was another Winnipegger, Ambrose J. Moran. The name of Amby Moran elicited some polite tut-tutting from Winnipeg parents. Amby missed part of a Western Canada League season because he was serving time in a Brandon jail for slugging a constable who had arrested him for being alcoholically enflamed in a public place.

Not long after the triumphal return of the Winnipeg Falcons, we moved from our house on Donald Street and became permanent residents of the Royal Alexandra Hotel. Far removed from the River Rinks at the foot of Kennedy Street, it was necessary to find new outlets for my hockey enthusiasm.

Unwittingly, even then I was preparing myself for a long career of second-guessing from the press box. The employees of the Royal Alexandra had a rag-tag hockey team with membership in the CPR house-league, which played weekly double-headers at the Amphitheatre. The employees permitted me to hang around and, with their tongues in their cheeks, they appointed me unofficial "manager" at the age of ten.

We had a terrible team. I don't remember much about the personnel beyond the fact that Dave Alexander, a middle-aged porter, was the exceptionally courageous goalie. Our self-appointed star was a voluble French waiter, named Jacquet, who had a Gallic flair for histrionics.

In the dressing room at the Amphitheatre, Jacquet would drape a large Royal Alexandra bedroom blanket over his shoulders, in preparation for going onto the ice. As he stepped from the players' box, it was my duty to remove the blanket from his shoulders with a flourish. This always elicited a chorus of boos from the few spectators who, because the flamboyant Jacquet had long sideburns and a head of curly black hair, referred to him loudly and derisively as "The Sheik."

I have vivid memories of one game in which our Royal Alexandra sad sacks played against the CPR Shops, a team of steam fitters, mechanics and other burly citizens who had more-than-average athletic ability. The star of the Shops was Andy Mulligan, who afterwards went on to a long and successful career in minor league professional hockey at Toledo, Ohio.

Late in the third period, Mulligan became bored with bombarding the luckless Dave Alexander. He broke through our porous defence, faked a shot at Alexander and then skated clear around our net. Without breaking stride, he skated all the way down to the other end of the rink and shot the puck past his own startled goalie. I remember the score; we were outlucked, 13-1. Mulligan saved us from a shutout.

The Royal Alexandra staff tolerated my presence only because they were working for a CPR hotel and my father's presence was a constant reminder of the source of their monthly pay-cheques. It was my father who persuaded the Royal Alex management to permit Jacquet and me to flood a vacant lot directly behind the hotel. Our efforts to have our own rink were fruitless. One afternoon, when we were attempting to make ice, the temperature dropped to minus 30 and we nearly froze to death. Our enthusiasm for the project ended — right there!

Fortunately, we had family friends over in the Fort Rouge area, whose grounds were so spacious that they built open-air rinks for their children. My school-friend, Bob Rogers, lived on Roslyn Road, and right next door to the Rogers' residence lived the Oslers, who had their own rink. After school, I would take my skates and hockey equipment to the Rogers' house where I'd change into combat uniform on a back stairway. Then we'd spend the rest of the afternoon playing shinny on the Osler rink.

Bob Rogers decreed that the Rogers children, the Osler children, the Gooderham children and I should adopt the uniforms of the Winnipeg Victorias. We went to Ashdown's Hardware on Main Street, where our indulgent parents bought us dark blue jerseys and toques with maroon trim. The official symbol of the Victorias, a red buffalo, was emblazoned on the left chest of the jersey.

On days when the elder Oslers tired of having their front lawn rink monopolized by yelping children, we would play shinny on the Gooderham family's private rink over on Wellington Crescent. I confess that I looked forward to playing at the Gooderhams' because I knew that Mr. Gooderham had four season tickets to every senior amateur hockey game which was played at the Amphitheatre.

Unblushingly, I acknowledge that I was a born conniver who would go to great lengths to be taken to a hockey game. My schoolmate, John Gooderham, usually fell in with my schemes. Hospitably, he would ask me to stay for supper after we had finished playing shinny. While we were eating, I would needle him to ask his father to take us to that night's hockey game.

Harry Gooderham was a very kind and patient gentleman. He sacrificed many evenings taking two small boys to a hockey game when, I'm quite sure, he would have preferred to remain at home, sitting in front of a roaring fire.

You may wonder, since my father was such an avid sports fan, why I didn't induce him to take me to all those hockey games. The explanation is simple: at that time, my father was vice-president of the Canadian Pacific's western region, which extended all the way from Fort William, Ontario, to Victoria, B.C. The vast size of that territory necessitated his absence from Winnipeg on business trips, which frequently lasted for two or three weeks. Indeed, when he was in town, he took us to as many hockey games as he could attend personally, particularly the Wednesday night double-headers in The Big Four Commercial League at the Amphitheatre.

The Big Four was composed of teams from the CPR, CNR, Eaton's and Hudson's Bay. The Big Four really was something! Until I moved to the press boxes of the NHL, it produced the best, most competitive hockey that I ever watched on a regular weekly basis.

By an amazing coincidence, every outstanding hockey player in Manitoba appeared to have become at least a part-time employee of one of those four corporations during the winter months. The eligibility rules may have been strained slightly; however, no team protested since all four were equally culpable of minor skulduggery. For instance, Andy Blair (later a star with the

Toronto Maple Leafs) was a law student at the University of Manitoba, but he played for CPR because he was a part-time employee in the local legal offices of the railway.

For the members of my family, the great attractions in the Big Four were those games between the arch rivals of transportation, the CPR and CNR.

One night, along with hundreds of CPR employees, I was screaming my lungs out, apparently for a lost cause. At the end of the second period, CNR was leading, 4-2. My father, who was a very dignified man, had been sitting beside me, seemingly oblivious to my juvenile screeching. Suddenly, midway through the final period, our CPR players found inspiration. Rousing themselves magnificently, they scored three goals within two minutes to lead the game, 5-4. As the third of those goals went into the CNR net, my father stood up abruptly. He raised his hat in the air and, quite loudly, shouted one word, "Hooray!" Then, just as abruptly, he sat down again. He didn't utter another word throughout the remainder of the game as CPR went on to a satisfactory 6-4 victory.

My father indulged me scandalously, and I have been forever grateful for his indulgence. Better than anyone, he realized that I never would be a hockey player. However, he detected the possibility that my passion for the sport could be channelled into some useful endeavour.

Without telling me, he continued to arrange things so that, at every opportunity, I was exposed to the best hockey in the world. When I first went to McGill University, "Red" Dutton was playing for the Montreal Maroons in the National Hockey League. He was the son of my father's friend, William A. Dutton. When the NHL season opened, I received a telephone call from "Red" at my boarding house. He said that he had two tickets for me for the Maroons' opening home-game.

Thereafter, "Red" Dutton arranged that two tickets would be available to me for any Maroon game. On top of that, he arranged for me to get tickets to the Montreal Canadiens' home-games. I didn't ask for any explanations of his generosity to a college freshman. I knew my father was behind it.

There were other hockey friends from Winnipeg in the NHL. During the years when Bob Rogers, John Gooderham and I were persuading our parents to buy us hockey equipment at Ashdown's Hardware, a young man named Charlie Gardiner worked there in the sporting goods department. That's the same Charlie Gardiner, the Chicago goalie, who, if he had lived longer, might have been the greatest goalie of all time.

That explains why I was standing behind the Chicago Black Hawk bench in the Montreal Forum when the Hawks played the Montreal Canadiens in the Stanley Cup semifinal in 1930. Charlie Gardiner persuaded Chicago coach Dick Irvin to let me act as the Black Hawk stickboy for that big game. There was another explanation: Dick Irvin's brother, Alex, was a CPR trainman back in Winnipeg, and he had been playing-coach of the CPR team in the Big Four League.

It was perhaps inevitable that I would make my way to the press boxes of the NHL. My father didn't help me, there. But I'm sure it didn't surprise him. He knew that if there was a good hockey game being played anywhere on this planet, I'd find some way of getting into the arena "on a pass."

The Winnipeg Falcons aboard the R.M.S. Grampian en route to the 1920 Olympic Games in Antwerp, Belgium. *Public Archives Canada/* PA 111330

3 THE OLYMPICS, 1920-1984

AFTER THE WINNIPEG FALCONS ESTABLISHED AN INTERNATIONAL reputation for Canadian hockey at Antwerp in 1920, Canadian teams went on to win five of the next six Winter Olympic tournaments, up to and including 1952. There was, of course, no Olympic competition in the War Years of 1940 and 1944.

No one in this country suspected that, when the Edmonton Mercurys picked up their gold medals at Oslo, Norway, in 1952, they would be the last Canadians to win an Olympic championship for more than 35 years.

The Edmonton Mercurys deserve a special mention in our sporting history, but the lamentable truth is that, beyond the bounds of Alberta's capital, their exploits have been forgotten by the great majority of their fellow-countrymen.

Minor league professional hockey had become the chief object of fan attention for Albertans in 1951 when Edmonton and Calgary joined the Pacific Coast League. This move effectively destroyed senior amateur hockey in the province's two major cities. Although the Mercurys played in a provincial intermediate league, in 1950 they had been considered strong enough to represent Canada at the world tournament in London, England. Indeed, they won the championship.

Nonetheless, when they were selected for the 1952 Olympics, the announcement received scant attention in other parts of Canada. Dr. W.G. Hardy, professor of classics at the University of Alberta and president of the International Ice Hockey Federation from 1948 through 1951, had been responsible for the Mercurys' invitation to the world tournament of 1950, and it is reasonable to assume that Dr. Hardy also espoused their cause as Olympic representatives in 1952.

Some idea of the public indifference can be taken from the fact that the *Edmonton Journal* — the only daily newspaper in the city at the time — didn't bother to send a reporter to Oslo with the Mercurys. Admittedly, the Mercurys were going on a tour, the length of which militated against any reporter's chances of accompanying the hockey team with expense account privileges. The Mercurys were away from home for four months, during which they were shuttled all over Europe, playing a total of 50 games and winning 45 of them.

As the results of the Mercurys' many exhibition matches drifted back to Canada, they did little to arouse national enthusiasm. In fact, when the Mercurys finally arrived in Oslo for the Olympic tournament, the only Canadian reporter on the scene was Jack Sullivan, sports editor of The Canadian Press news agency.

The Edmonton Mercurys really were amateurs, in the financial sense. During their four-month tour, the Canadian Amateur Hockey Association provided each member of the party with only $25 per week for expenses. The team subsisted on a small share of the gate-receipts from their exhibition games and, more specifically, they depended on the personal largesse of James Christiensen, an automobile dealer in Edmonton. Christiensen sold Ford products at Waterloo Motors, hence the Mercury nickname for his hockey team.

The Edmonton automobile dealer looked after some financial obligations for players who, due to the length of the tour, had to take leaves-of-absence from their regular jobs. He paid the players' regular weekly wages to the wives of those who were married. He was reputed to have paid $30,000 out of his own pocket to finance the Mercurys' 1950 world tournament trip. And he is also said to have forked over another $100,000 for their 1952 tour.

The IOC officials had performed their customary crafty job of seeding the nine countries who competed for the 1952 championship. With their usual prescience, they had decreed that Canada and the United States would meet in the final game of the round robin.

To the surprise of no one, Canada came up to that final match with a record of seven wins and no losses. The United States team was ensconced firmly in second place with a record of six wins and one loss. The Americans had stumbled in their very first game, losing to Sweden, 2-4.

Thus, Canada needed only a tie in the final game to take the gold medals. That's the way the tournament ended — in a 3-3 tie!

Canada was leading, 2-0, on goals by Bill Dawe and Lou Secco, in the early going. But the Americans struggled back with goals by Johnny Mulhern and Ruben Bjorkman. Then, before the end of the second period, Canada went ahead, again, on a goal by Don Gauf. However, the Americans earned a draw when Jimmy Sedin scored for them before full-time.

Back home in Canada, the reports of the Olympic tournament were accepted with a dangerous bit of smug boredom. To our lasting chagrin, we still were saying in those days: "Ho hum! We got away with sending a team of intermediates to beat those European humpty-dumpties." Little did we suspect the frequent come-uppances that were in store for us in the ensuing 35 years.

The Mercurys may have been ignored in other parts of Canada, but they came home to a tumultuous welcome in Edmonton. The mayor of the city was the extroverted Bill Hawrelak. Always on the lookout for a good publicity gimmick, he decreed a Day of Welcome for the hockey team. The Mercurys were paraded through the midtown streets in a motorcade and honoured in a ceremony at City Hall. In one exciting day, their fellow-Edmontonians made up for the indifference that the hockey players had received in other parts of the country.

I confess that, where the Mercurys were concerned, I shared the general Canadian indifference in 1952. Although I was a hockey nut, I couldn't exult over a victory by a team of intermediates. Some of the Mercury names were familiar to me — Don Gauf, Bill Dawe, Bob Watt and George Abel — but reports on Alberta intermediate hockey seldom sifted through to Toronto, where I was working at the time.

Louis Holmes, the Edmonton coach, had been a longtime favourite of mine. I had known him almost 20 years earlier when he was playing minor league professional hockey. Louis also had a brief National Hockey League career with the Chicago Black Hawks and the Detroit Red Wings.

In fact, it was Holmes who inspired one of my best-loved stories about oldtime professional hockey publicists. When Louis joined the Black Hawks, the team's publicist was Joe Farrell, an archetypical, cigar-smoking, whiskey-drinking newspaperman from the gaudiest era of Chicago journalism. Farrell was one of those publicists who seldom permitted the dull truth to interfere with his own imagination when he got around to writing press releases for the Chicago hockey reporters.

Louis Holmes was a magnificently smooth and seemingly effortless skater. At his first Black Hawk practice, his skating style immediately attracted the attention of reporters, and the newspapermen asked Farrell for some background material on this promising young player from Edmonton. With a wicked gleam in his eye, old Joe sat down at his typewriter and he produced a little bit of journalistic fantasy.

Farrell wrote that the amazing skating ability of Louis Holmes was due to the fact that, back home, Louis was a postman who in the winter delivered the weekly mail from Edmonton to Grande Prairie, *skating* all the way over the frozen North Saskatchewan River.

Chicago newspapermen knew very little about Canada's geography or culture. One Chicago daily printed Farrell's press release without bothering to change even a comma.

Several years after the Holmes story, the first of the Bentley brothers, Doug, arrived in Chicago to play for the Hawks.

One night, Bentley was indisposed and Farrell, in a press release explaining his absence from the lineup, wrote: "Young Bentley is suffering from painfully stretched neck muscles. Yesterday, he was gawking upwards at all the Chicago skyscrapers. Before coming to Chicago, Bentley never had seen a building which was taller than three storeys."

In Joe Farrell's day, professional hockey players were paid small salaries. Generally speaking, they had a good deal of fun and they didn't take themselves seriously. Five decades later, professional hockey players won't move a muscle without consulting their lawyer-agents; they are interested primarily in long-term contracts at astronomically high salaries and, instead of reading nonsense, such as that produced by old Joe Farrell, they read *The Wall Street Journal*.

In retrospect, that final Olympic triumph of the Edmonton Mercurys in 1952, brings at least one pertinent fact into sharp perspective. The Europeans had never seen Canada's best hockey players! Canada's 150 top hockey players performed in the NHL. The teams that we sent to the Olympics or world tournaments represented a level of performer who, for the most part, couldn't "make" the NHL.

Ironically, our first Olympic teams, in the 1920s, were distinct departures from the norm of the next four decades. My personal heroes, the Winnipeg Falcons of 1920, had three players — Frank Fredrickson, "Slim" Haldarson and Bobby Benson — who later played in the NHL. Fredrickson, an early superstar, was later enshrined in the Hockey Hall of Fame in Toronto.

W.A. Hewitt, father of Hall of Fame broadcaster Foster Hewitt, accompanied the Falcons to Antwerp as honorary team manager. In his autobiography, *Down the Stretch*, he recalled the extraordinary circumstances in which the pioneering Winnipeg team made the trip.

The 1920 Summer Olympics had been awarded to Antwerp and, early in that year, the Belgian city decided to stage some winter sports championships. The major sports in this somewhat informal schedule were figure-skating, speed-skating and ice hockey. Quite casually, the Belgians invited Canada to send a hockey team.

The Canadian Amateur Hockey Association was mulling over this invitation while the Allan Cup finals were being played in Toronto. The Falcons had travelled east with nothing on their minds but those finals in which they gave a waxing to the Toronto Eatons.

The CAHA decided to ask the Falcons to travel to Antwerp. They didn't even have time to return to Winnipeg for a post-Allan Cup civic reception. The CAHA issued each of the eight players with $25 "to purchase haberdashery," and, shoving their soiled shirts into their suitcases, the Winnipeg Icelanders rushed to Saint John, New Brunswick, where they boarded an ocean liner for Europe. They didn't even have time to bid adieu to their families. As Hewitt points out in his book, no hockey player in 1920 would have dreamed of making a long-distance telephone call from Toronto to Winnipeg — not even to tell his wife that he wouldn't be home for another month. He expected her to read the sports pages.

Those first Olympic hockey matches were held in a small artificial-ice rink, which was the headquarters of a figure-skating club. The ice-surface was only 170 feet long and 70 feet wide, but the Canadians adapted quickly. After all, most of them had learned to skate on small open-air corner-lot rinks in Manitoba.

The Falcons were required to play only three games at Antwerp. They defeated Czechoslovakia, 15-1, and they outscored Sweden, 12-1. Even in that very first Olympic tournament, though, the United States clearly was second-best. The Americans played excellent hockey, holding the Falcons to a 2-0 score.

It is interesting to note that the American star in 1920 was defenceman Frank "Moose" Goheen from St. Paul, Minnesota. Goheen was one of the first American-born players ever to be inducted into the Hockey Hall of Fame. He played professional hockey, but not in the NHL.

Hewitt wrote that, although Frank Fredrickson was the elegant star of the Falcons, the Canadian who fascinated the European crowds in that little Antwerp arena was Mike Goodman, the speed-skater. The Europeans had never seen anyone who could cover the ice so swiftly. Mike performed with such dazzling speed that the crowds suspected him of having some form of jet propulsion in his skates. Hewitt reported that Goodman was offered $100 to

Above: The Toronto Granites, 1924. *Hockey Hall of Fame*
Below: The Toronto Granites at the 1924 Winter Olympics, Chamonix, Switzerland. *Hockey Hall of Fame*

sell his boots and blades to a pioneering European hockey-promoter who wished to solve the secret of Mike's high-velocity capers.

Canada's next Olympic team, the Toronto Granites of 1924, produced several players who had distinguished careers in the NHL. Dunc Munro, captain of the Granites, captained the Montreal Maroons when they won the Stanley Cup in 1926 and later became playing-coach of that team. Bert McCaffery, the Granite right-winger, played for Toronto, the Montreal Canadiens and Pittsburgh in the NHL. Beattie Ramsay played for Toronto. Reginald J. "Hooley" Smith, centreman for the Granites, had an NHL career which led him to induction into the Hockey Hall of Fame. He turned professional with the Ottawa Senators and he was with them when they won the Stanley Cup for the last time in 1927. "Hooley" was traded to the Montreal Maroons, where he had many outstanding seasons at right wing on Montreal's famed "Three S Line" with Nelson Stewart and Albert "Babe" Siebert.

It is just possible that those Toronto Granites who went to the 1924 Winter Olympics in Chamonix, France, were the best amateur team to represent Canada at the international level. They had two good goaltenders: Jack

Cameron and Ernie Collett. Beattie Ramsay partnered Dunc Munro on defence. Harry Watson played left wing on the forward line with Smith and McCaffery.

To that seven-man squad, the Granites added only two players for their trip to Europe. To soothe the sensibilities of clamorous hockey fans in other sections of the country, the Granites picked up young Harold McMunn from the Winnipeg Falcons and Sig Slater, a veteran centre from the Montreal Victorias. The coach of the Toronto team was Frank Rankin. W.A. Hewitt made another trip to Europe as official baby-sitter.

The Olympic tournament at Chamonix was played on an open-air rink. The side-boards around the playing surface were only about 12 inches high, and the spectators had to be nimble to avoid being decapitated by flying pucks.

Eight countries were hockey participants at Chamonix. The bigdomes of the planning committee seeded Canada and the United States in two separate four-team divisions, in anticipation that they would meet for the gold medals.

The tournament developed according to plan, but no one anticipated the tremendous scores that would be run up by the Granites. In the preliminary round, Canada swamped Czechoslovakia, 30-0; Sweden, 22-0; and Switzerland, 33-0. Then, in a semifinal match, Canada defeated Britain, 19-2. Although the Americans gave a good account of themselves in the final, they simply couldn't cope with the all-round efficiency of the Granites and were defeated, 6-1.

The Granites filled their hats at Chamonix. They scored the amazing total of 110 goals in five games, and they yielded a total of only three goals. Harry Watson led the Canadians with 38 goals. Their other scorers were Bert McCaffery (22), "Hooley" Smith (18), Dunc Munro (16), Beattie Ramsay (10), Harold McMunn (3) and Sig Slater (3).

Dunc Munro recalled that, during one preliminary game, he looked behind him and realized that no one was guarding the Canadian net. Goalie Jack Cameron had skated over to the low boards near the blueline, and he was having an exceptionally animated chat with two young ladies.

It is interesting to note that W.A. Hewitt, who accompanied Canada's teams to every Olympic tournament from 1920 through 1936, expressed the opinion in his autobiography that our dominance of international hockey attained its zenith in 1928, when our representatives were the Toronto Varsity Grads. Hewitt's opinion is unassailable, in view of his lifetime as one of Canada's most important hockey officials. However, it is difficult to imagine how the Varsity Grads could have been much superior to those Toronto Granites — a team that ran up such tremendous scores and whose lineup included so many players who became outstanding professionals. Probably, Hewitt surmised that the opposition which the Varsity Grads faced in 1928 was considerably superior to the teams that the Granites annihilated in 1924. It should be pointed out, though, that the Americans weren't at St. Moritz to oppose the Varsity Grads in 1928.

Certainly, the Varsity Grads had a great team, but only one of their players, Dave Trottier, went to the NHL, to play for many years for the Montreal

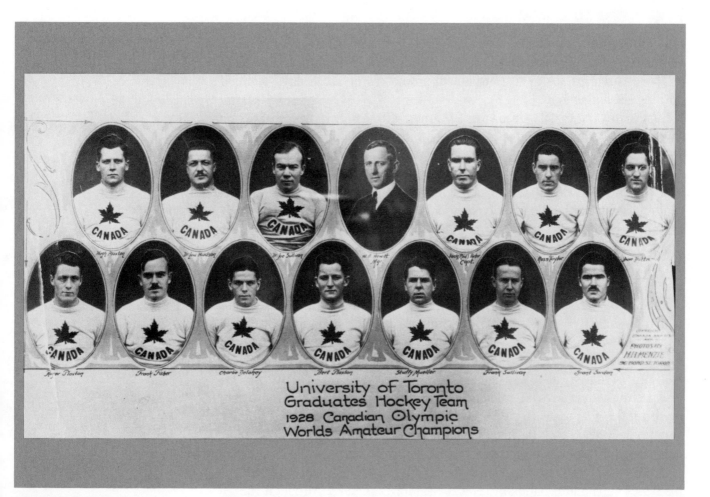

University of Toronto
Graduates Hockey Team
1928 Canadian Olympic
Worlds Amateur Champions

Most of the 1928 Varsity Grads became members of the Toronto business and professional Establishment.
Public Archives Canada/ PA 49634

Maroons. Although many of the other Varsity Grads were good enough for the NHL, in Canada in the 1920s, there was a certain amount of snobbery connected with a university education. To be blunt about it: in 1928, college graduates were expected to aspire to better circumstances than labour among the peons in a professional sport. The exceptions to the general rule were Trottier and two University of Manitoba graduates: Murray Murdoch, who played with the New York Rangers, and Andy Blair, who played for the Toronto Maple Leafs.

I have vivid memories of the Varsity Grads because my father arranged for my release from boarding school in Victoria to watch them meet Fort William in the 1927 Allan Cup finals at Vancouver. As a western chauvinist, I was deflated when the Grads made short work of Fort William. I consoled myself with the thought that it might have been a better-contested series if Eric Pettinger, Fort William's centreman, hadn't broken a wrist in the Western Canada playoffs. In Pettinger's absence, the Fort William mantle of leadership fell on the shoulders of Jimmy Ward, who later played for the Montreal Maroons for more than a decade. Pettinger also became a pro with the Toronto Maple Leafs.

The Olympic organizers were in a quandary when the United States declined to send a team to St. Moritz, Switzerland. Cudgelling their massive brains, the officials devised a scheme under which Canada would sit idle while nine other countries, divided into three groups, would scuffle among themselves to produce three group-winners. Then Canada would play the winners of those three groups. The tournament-promoters of those days were, if nothing else, ingenious.

Eventually, the Varsity Grads met the group-winners: Sweden, Britain and Switzerland. Canada defeated Sweden, 11-0; Britain, 14-0; and Switzerland, 13-0.

This was the first time Canada had dispatched a large squad of players to Europe. The 1928 Varsity Grads had 13 men in their lineup at St. Moritz. The goaltenders were Dr. Joe Sullivan and Norbert "Stuffy" Mueller. Their defencemen were John "Red" Porter, Ross Taylor, Frank W. Fisher and Roger Plaxton. Their starting forward line had Hugh Plaxton at centre with Dave Trottier and Dr. Lou Hudson on the wings. Their substitute forwards were Frank Sullivan, Charlie Delahaye, Bert Plaxton and Grant Gordon.

Most of the Varsity Grads went on to prominence in the Toronto business and professional Establishment. Joe Sullivan became a nationally distinguished otolaryngologist and was appointed to the Senate of Canada. Frank Fisher was a senior partner in the law firm of Ludwig, Holness and Fisher. Lou Hudson, a dentist, also was a licensed pilot with an interest in mineral prospecting. A few days after defenceman Bill Barilko became a Toronto hero by firing the goal that defeated the Montreal Canadiens in the 1951 Stanley Cup final, Hudson took Barilko in his plane on a prospecting trip. The plane crashed in Ontario bush-country and both men were killed.

A man who was to become a persistent gadfly in professional hockey made his debut on the international scene at St. Moritz in 1928. Although Harold Ballard, of Toronto, had no official connection with the Canadian delegation, he turned up in Switzerland and contrived to carry the Canadian flag when the athletes from the competing nations marched into the open-air stadium for the opening ceremonies. W.A. Hewitt, in his autobiography, recalled kindly that "young Harold Ballard was very helpful."

The experiences of 1924 and 1928 lulled Canadian hockey men into a state of false security. The country, generally, was unprepared for the shocks that were to hit them in the next decade. First came the Olympic Games of 1932, which left the handwriting on the wall. Canadians had become grossly overconfident where their southern neighbours were concerned, completely forgetting that the Americans hadn't bothered to compete at St. Moritz in 1928. The 1932 Olympics at Lake Placid, New York, came perilously close to being a disaster for Canada.

As far as the American hosts were concerned, their Olympic hockey tournament was less than a spectacular financial success. The year, 1932, was the nadir of the worldwide economic depression. As a result, only two European countries — Germany and Poland — felt wealthy enough to send teams to North America for the hockey spiel. Canada and the U.S.A. brought the tournament complement to only four teams.

Canada's representatives were the Winnipegs from my hometown. I was, by then, a student at McGill University, and it distressed me to read the eastern newspapers, which were trashing the poor Winnipegs in print long before the Olympic tournament began.

The Winnipegs had won the Allan Cup in 1931, defeating the Hamilton Tigers in the national final. Honesty compels me to acknowledge that, even in Winnipeg, this team had become known affectionately but also derisively as "The Scoreless Wonders." The Winnipegs were speedy skaters who had perfected back-checking as a fine art, but they couldn't put the puck in the other team's net. A typical game score for them was: Winnipegs 1, Opponents 0.

Possibly, 1931 hadn't been a vintage year for Canadian senior hockey. The only pro to emerge from the Allan Cup finals was Hector "Toe" Blake of Hamilton. Blake went to one Stanley Cup victory as a player with the Montreal Maroons, three more Stanley Cups as a player with the Montreal Canadiens, and then he coached Les Canadiens to a record eight triumphs in Stanley Cup competition.

Thus, long before the Winnipegs turned up at Lake Placid, they were being criticized noisily. The eastern reporters pointed out, *ad nauseum*, that Canada was stupid to repose its Olympic aspirations in a team which had averaged only slightly more than two goals per game throughout the entire previous season.

Yielding to pressure from the Canadian Amateur Hockey Association, the Winnipegs made some additions before they left for Lake Placid. They picked up two outstanding forwards from the Selkirk Fishermen — Walter Monson and Norm Malloy — but Coach Jack Hughes made it abundantly clear that he wasn't going to have "any censored-censored Easterners" foisted on him.

Those were the first Olympics I had ever witnessed. Even then, Lake Placid was only a drive of a couple of hours from Montreal. But I had an uncomfortable feeling in my stomach when our own McGill team went down to Lake Placid to play a couple of pre-Olympic exhibition games. McGill defeated the U.S., 2-0, and then, exhibiting commendable impartiality, beat Canada, 2-1. The outlook was rather gruesome.

With only four countries represented, the officials decided on a double round-robin tournament for the first and only time in Olympic history. The low-scoring Winnipegs didn't have much trouble with Germany or Poland, but the Americans were a different matter. The first time the two teams met, the game went into overtime and Canada won, 2-1, when "Hack" Simpson finally shot the puck into the U.S. net. The second game was even more agonizing for supporters of the Canadian cause. After the teams played *three* overtime periods, the score was still tied, 2-2. Canada was awarded the gold medals because the Americans hadn't managed to defeat them in either game.

That second game was a cliff hanger for Canada. With less than a minute left to play in regulation-time, the U.S. was leading, 2-1. "Hack" Simpson was dawdling through middle-ice with the puck when Coach Hughes screamed at him, "Move it! There are only 35 seconds to play!"

Simpson's retort reads like wildly improbable apocrypha, but so help me, it's the truth. Simpson shouted back, "That's lots of time!" With which he passed the puck to Romeo Rivers, who flipped it into the net for the goal that sent the game into overtime.

For the first time in four Olympics, Canada didn't have the leading scorer in the hockey tournament. Winthrop Palmer of the U.S. team topped the list with eight goals. Walter Monson was second with seven goals and "Hack" Simpson was third with six.

Of all the players in the 1932 tournament, Simpson was the only one to receive a nibble from the NHL. Although he was a fine stick-handler, he couldn't skate fast enough to cause a breeze. The Montreal Maroons used him for a few games, but, discouraged by his lack of celerity, they farmed him out to Windsor and later to Quebec. At the end of his first pro season, "Hack" was content to go home to a permanent job on the Winnipeg Grain Exchange.

In later years, the most famous graduate of the Winnipegs was Vic Lindquist, who became an outstanding referee. He officiated all across Canada in addition to serving frequently as a referee in world hockey tournaments.

There is a story about Lindquist officiating in Europe, in a world tournament game between Sweden and Czechoslovakia. The competing players knew only that Lindquist was a referee from Canada. In the very first period, Lindquist called a penalty against a Swede. The player accepted the penalty with a phony smile. As he was skating past the referee on his way to the box, he said in Swedish, "You blind son of a bitch." To the player's surprise, Lindquist replied, also in Swedish, "Young man, that will cost you a ten-minute misconduct penalty."

In retrospect, the warning signals had been flashing as early as 1920 when the Winnipeg Falcons were held to a 2-0 score by the Americans. Yet Canadians clung stubbornly to the belief that, in a crisis, our teams wouldn't lose. Accordingly, no Canadians were prepared for John Francis "Bunny" Ahearne's "putsch" at Garmisch-Partenkirchen, Germany, in 1936.

Even Canada's preparations for the 1936 Olympics were inauspicious. The Halifax Wolves won the Allan Cup in 1935 and were designated as the 1936 Olympic colour-bearers. However, before the 1935-36 hockey season began, several members of the Halifax club had jumped to other teams. Thereupon, the CAHA decreed that the Port Arthur Bearcats, who had been the defeated Allan Cup finalists in 1935, deserved the right to go to Garmisch.

Warned by the near-defeat of the Winnipegs in 1932, the CAHA took the precaution of adding five good Montreal players to the Port Arthur lineup for the Olympics. The additions were Herman Murray, Hugh Farquharson, Kenny Farmer, Dave Neville and the veteran Ralph St. Germain. Before leaving for Europe, goaltender Frank "Dinty" Moore, of Port Colborne, Ontario, also joined the team.

Meanwhile, "Bunny" Ahearne, a cocky little Irish conniver, had become general secretary of the British Ice Hockey Federation by 1933. He was on his way to becoming the dominant figure in international hockey. An early biographer described Ahearne as "capable of acting unscrupulously in pursuit of his own advantage." That was one of the milder assessments to be made of him in the next 40 years.

Ahearne was singularly wily, as well as unscrupulous. "Bunny" had a "mole" working somewhere in the registry office of the Canadian Amateur Hockey Association. By 1934, Ahearne had obtained a complete list of all Canadian-

Above: The Canadian Olympic team of 1936, the first Canadian team to not win first place at the Winter Olympics. *Hockey Hall of Fame*
J.F. "Bunny" Ahearne, General Secretary of the British Ice Hockey Federation in 1936. *Hockey Hall of Fame*

registered players who had been born in the British Isles. Most of those players had been brought to Canada as babies by their parents. In all cases, they had received all their hockey training and development in Canada.

Even his detractors acknowledge that Ahearne was a Machiavellian strategist. The Canadian Prairies were deep in the economic depression in the early 1930s, and "Bunny" had no difficulty in luring good hockey players from stony-broke Winnipeg to perform in his London & District League, where they received as much as $50 per week. This was a small fortune, compared to the money that could be obtained on the Prairies.

Percy Nicklin, who had coached the Moncton Hawks to two successive Allan Cup victories in 1933 and 1934, was induced to go to England to coach the Harringay Racers. In preparation for 1936, Ahearne chose Nicklin to coach Britain's Olympic Team.

"Bunny" went to Garmisch with a squad, the backbone of which was eight ersatz Britons, all of whom had been imported from Canada. The star of the British side was Jimmy Foster, who is remembered in his prairie hometown as one of the two greatest goaltenders ever to come out of Winnipeg. (The other was Charlie Gardiner, the Hall of Famer who backstopped the Chicago Black Hawks to their first Stanley Cup triumph.) The other Canadian-developed players on the British team were: defenceman Gordon Dailley, from Winnipeg; centre Jimmy Chappell, from Whitby, Ontario; right-winger Alex Archer, from Winnipeg; Gerry Davey, from Port Arthur, Ontario; Edgar "Chirp" Brenchley, from Niagara Falls; Archie Stinchcombe, from Windsor; and Harry Pyefinch, from Ottawa.

February 11, 1936, is remembered as a day of infamy by Canadian hockey fans.

In a semifinal match, Gerry Davey, a "Briton" from Port Arthur, shot the puck into the Canadian net after only 20 seconds of play. Then Jimmy Foster gave one of the most amazing goaltending displays of his entire career as the Canadians attacked relentlessly. Foster yielded one goal to Ralph St. Germain at 12:30 of the first period, but that was all the scoring the frustrated Canadians could manage. At 12:48 of the third period, "Chirp" Brenchley scored Britain's winning goal after Gordon Dailley had picked up a loose puck while the Canadians were swarming inside the British blueline.

But that wasn't to be the worst of it. Canada fully expected to get another crack at the Brits in the four-team final round. The team never got its second chance. Ahearne insisted that, because Britain had beaten Canada once, a return match in the final wasn't necessary.

The uproar was so furious that Paul Loicq of Belgium, the president of the International Ice Hockey Federation, was obliged to call an emergency meeting to deal with Canada's protests. Ahearne outmanoeuvred the Canadians. When the vote came, five countries, including the U.S.A., sided with Ahearne. Canada's only supporter was Germany.

Britain received the gold medals, although over the entire tournament they had played one less game than the Canadians — eight games for Canada and seven games for Britain. Canada's complete tournament record was seven wins and one loss. Britain's complete tournament record was five wins and two ties.

Ahearne walked away, laughing. Particularly galling to hockey-men in this country was the fact that Canada had not only been beaten on the ice but had also been outsmarted at the IIHF conference table.

Throughout the remainder of his long career in the IIHF, Ahearne appeared to take particular delight in upsetting the Canadians. Usually, he was successful. In those circumstances, it was a bit surprising — to say the least — when the selection committee, composed almost entirely of Canadians, voted him into the Hockey Hall of Fame at Toronto in 1977. Although I had occasion to know Ahearne in later years, nothing that he did in his old age appeared to qualify him for the honour of enshrinement in a Hall of Fame that was, primarily, a Canadian institution. Possibly, the Canadian members of the selection committee "turned the other cheek" just a bit too readily. "Bunny" was a lively and entertaining individual but even his European colleagues conceded readily that he was a double-dealing, self-serving little rascal from the opening face-off to the final buzzer.

An incident which occurred during the 1952 Olympics in Oslo illustrates the intense animosity that Ahearne always managed to arouse in Canadian hockey-men. On the eve of the championship game, after a stormy meeting of IIHF delegates, Doug Grimston, the CAHA president from British Columbia, became involved in an argument with Ahearne in a hotel lobby. The confrontation became so heated that Grimston threw a punch at Ahearne. "Bunny" ducked the punch and fled up a flight of stairs. He was pursued by Grimston who, in turn, was pursued by Jack Sullivan, sports editor of The Canadian Press, who was intent on preventing bloodshed. At the top of the stairs, Ahearne turned and kicked Grimston in the belly. Grimston fell backwards down the stairs, upending Sullivan, the luckless pacifist. "Bunny" escaped unscathed, leaving the Canadians in a state of embarrassment.

In our young, relatively unsophisticated and economically depressed country, that 1936 Olympic hockey defeat was a demoralizing blow. In the bleak months which followed, we were forced to wring some small consolation from the realization that the Brits probably couldn't have won that championship without the services of the eight Canadians in their lineup.

Infinitely more important problems were to occupy the attention of Canadians throughout the next decade, and Olympic competitions weren't resumed until 1948.

For those first post-war Olympics at St. Moritz, Canada sent an air force team known as the RCAF Flyers. They were coached by Frank Boucher, Jr., a son of George "Buck" Boucher, the oldest of four famous brothers who performed in the NHL. Young Frank attached the "Junior" to his name to avoid being confused with his uncle, Frank Boucher, who was still coaching the New York Rangers.

The Flyers were a solid team, but not knowing what type of competition would be awaiting them in St. Moritz, the CAHA decided to strengthen the squad by adding two outstanding amateur players from Toronto — Wally

Above: The R.C.A.F. Flyers, Canada's 1948 Olympic gold medal winners. *Hockey Hall of Fame* Below: The R.C.A.F. Flyers in action. *Public Archives Canada/PA 108276*

Halder and George Mara. Those two recruits proved to be the individual stars of the tournament; Halder scored 21 goals and Mara, 17.

The hockey team played second fiddle at those 1948 Olympics. The outstanding Canadian at St. Moritz was Barbara Ann Scott, the petite blond figure-skater from Ottawa. Scott was wildly acclaimed as she added the Olympic title to her previously won world championship. She attached herself to the hockey squad as their official mascot, and the Flyers responded by winning the hockey championship.

Canada and Czechoslovakia completed the tournament with identical records: seven wins and one tie. And, when the Canadians and the Czechs met, they played to a scoreless draw. Thereupon, the international officials went into consultation. They emerged to announce that Canada had won the gold medals because they had the best scoring differential: 69 goals for and 5 against. The Czechs were awarded the silver medals. Their scoring differential was 80 goals for and 18 against.

Next on the Olympic program came the win of the Edmonton Mercurys in 1952, followed by the Kitchener-Waterloo Dutchmen's trips to Cortina, Italy, in 1956, and Squaw Valley, Colorado, in 1960.

Those two squads from Kitchener-Waterloo, both coached by Bobby Bauer, the former Boston Bruin "Kraut Liner," were good hockey teams, but they didn't achieve their objectives in Olympic competition. They won the bronze medals at Cortina and they had to settle for the silver medals at Squaw Valley, where they were handcuffed by the brilliant goaltending of Jack McCartan of the United States.

The 1956 tournament featured the Olympic hockey debut of the Soviet Union. The Soviets had sent shock waves reverberating to North America in 1954 after their first appearance in major international competition — they thumped Canada's Toronto Lyndhursts, 7-2, in the world tournament at Moscow. The following year, Canada had been avenged by the Penticton Vees, who went to West Germany and shut out the Russians, 5-0.

The Edmonton Mercurys Hockey Club, 1952 Olympic champions. *Hockey Hall of Fame*

However, the prime objective of the Soviets had always been their first Olympic tournament, and, operating with their usual efficiency, they proved to be unbeatable in Cortina. They defeated Canada, 2-0, on the final day, after disposing of the United States, 4-0. Meanwhile, Canada had stumbled in an earlier game, losing to the Americans by a 4-1 score. As a result, the Americans picked up the silver medals while the Kitchener-Waterloo Dutchmen had to settle for third place.

For the 1960 tournament at Squaw Valley, Bobby Bauer's Kitchener team had been strengthened substantially by the addition of other players from eastern Canada. Among the recruits were Bobby Rousseau (later to be a member of the Stanley Cup-winning Montreal Canadien teams), Bob Attersley, Darryl Sly, George Semolenko and defenceman Harry Sinden. This was to be the only Olympic appearance for Sinden, who coached Team Canada in the 1972 Summit Series with the Soviets.

The Canadians were well prepared for Squaw Valley, but history suggests that they erred in their selection of major targets. Unquestionably, the team was intent on defeating the Russians. They accomplished this by whipping the Soviets, 8-5, in a free-scoring game. However, they may have underrated the Americans. With Jack McCartan giving one of the finest goaltending performances ever seen in Olympic competition, the U.S. defeated Canada, 2-1. McCartan, in his next game, held the Soviets to two goals while his teammates scored three.

The victory for the United States at Squaw Valley provided the first gold medals for the Americans, who had been trying to win them since their first team went to Brussels in 1920. After 40 years of waiting, they richly deserved their triumph.

Father David Bauer's National Team represented Canada at the Olympics of 1964 and 1968. Their activities are recorded in Chapter Four.

On January 4, 1970, Canada, angered by double-dealings within the Ahearne-dominated IIHF, withdrew from international hockey competition. For this reason, we didn't send teams to the 1972 Olympics in Japan or the 1976 Olympics in Austria.

In preparation for returning to Olympic play at Lake Placid, New York, in 1980, Canada assembled a revived version of the National Team with headquarters at The Corral in Calgary. To give the squad a truly national image, it was decided to appoint a staff of three coaches, all from different cities. The men selected were Clare Drake from Edmonton, Tom Watt from Toronto, and Lorne Davis from Winnipeg.

The 1980 revival was not spectacularly successful. Canada faded into the background early as the U.S. team stole the spotlight. Canada didn't even reach the four-team championship round. Although the Canadians had a second-period lead, they lost to the Soviets, 4-6. Even more disastrous had been Canada's 3-4 loss to Finland, the winning goal being scored on a 100-foot shot, which simply slid along the ice.

Meanwhile, the Americans, encouraged by the highly emotional crowds of their countrymen who jammed the Lake Placid Arena, were performing magnificently. In the championship round, they scored a sensational 4-3

Above: A superior Soviet team defeats Canada 6-4 at the 1980 Winter Olympics. *James Lipa* **Below: Paul MacLean, now with the Winnipeg Jets, moves in on goal in a 1980 Olympics game.** *James Lipa*

victory over the startled Soviets before wrapping up the Olympic title by defeating Finland. However, the *pièce de résistance* was the victory over the Russians. That was the most satisfactory day in the history of American hockey — even more exhilarating than their triumph at Squaw Valley in 1960.

Canada's preparations for the 1984 Winter Olympics at Sarajevo, Yugoslavia, were considerably more painstaking than the hurried-up program for 1980. As chairman of Hockey Canada's International Committee, Sam Pollock asked for a new coaching staff, composed of Dave King, Jean Perron and George Kingston. King, who had been very successful at the University of Saskatchewan, had also coached Canada to the gold medals in the 1982 world junior championships.

King, who is now general manager as well as head coach of the National Team, has devoted a good deal of his time over the past five years attempting to persuade NHL clubs to permit him to make use of young players who have been drafted by the professionals. Backed by Pollock, he has argued passionately that, if those young players are allowed to get a year or two of international hockey experience on the National Team, they will be better prepared for their eventual debuts in the major professional league.

Team Canada '84 went to the Olympic Games at Sarajevo with high hopes, but only 24 hours before their opening game, they were dealt a serious blow. The International Hockey Committee ruled that Canada must drop Mark Morrison and Don Dietrich from the lineup. Morrison had played nine games with the New York Rangers two seasons earlier, while Dietrich had been with the Chicago Black Hawks during the 1983-84 season.

Left: J.J. Daigneault in a Canada-U.S. game at the 1984 Winter Olympics. *James Lipa* Opposite: Celebrating a goal at a 1984 Olympics match. *James Lipa*

Deprived of those two players, King's team still managed to perform rather creditably. They reached the four-team championship round, but had to settle for fourth place after they were beaten, 4-0, by the Soviets and, 2-0, by Sweden.

Still, as King and his present assistant, Guy Charron, prepare for the Calgary Olympics, they have much evidence to support their contention that a season or two in the National Team program provides admirable preparation for a player to move up to the NHL. Five players from the 1980 Olympic Team are active in the NHL. They are Glen Anderson and Randy Gregg of the Edmonton Oilers and three members of the Winnipeg Jets — Paul MacLean, Tim Watters and Jim Nill. From the 1984 National Team, the following 16 players moved up to the NHL: James Patrick, Pat Flatley, Mario Gosselin, Kirk Muller, Bruce Driver, Russ Courtnall, J.J. Daigneault, Carey Wilson, Doug Lidster, Michel Petit, Robin Bartel, Craig Redmond, Darren Eliott, Kevin Dineen, Dave Tippett and Dave Donnelly. Additionally, Jean Perron, who was University of New Brunswick coach before he assisted Dave King with the National Team in 1983 and 1984, moved up to be coach of the Montreal Canadiens, winning the Stanley Cup in his rookie NHL season.

On the eve of the 1988 Olympics, King and his players are anticipating that their secret weapon will be a tremendous outpouring of emotional support from the pro-Canadian crowd in Calgary's Olympic Saddledome. Just as the pro-American crowds inspired the United States to a title at Lake Placid in 1980, they are hoping that unstinting fan approval will inspire a Canadian team to its first Olympic championship since 1952.

Canadian fans at the 1984 Winter Olympics at Sarajevo, Yugoslavia. *James Lipa*

Above: Canadian goaltender makes a save at the 1984 Olympics. *James Lipa*   Right: Dave Tippett scores against the U.S. in a 1984 Olympics game. *James Lipa*

R.J. KELLY *R.W.*

S.P.A. CUP

RICHARDSON TROPHY

MEMORIAL CUP

O.H.A. CUP

N.J. METZ *L.W.*

CLARENCE DROUILLARD *Centre*

T.R. BAUER *R.W.*

R.J. HAMILTON *R. Defense*

HARVEY TENO *Goal*

J.H. HAMILTON *L. Defense*

A.M. JACKSON *Centre*

JOHN ACHESON *L.W.*

J.J. BURKE *Defense*

St. Michael's College
Canadian Junior 1934 Champions

D.W. WILLSON *Defense*

LEO McLEAN *Goal*

J.J. TIMMONS *Manager*

DR. W.J. LAFLAMME *Coach*

REV. M.S. LYNCH *Director of Athletics*

HUGH GILROY

F.N. BAUER

THE NATIONAL TEAM, 1962-1970

4

THE MOST NOBLY CONCEIVED OF ALL CANADIAN HOCKEY ENTER-prises was the formation of the National Team, dedicated to refurbishing this country's somewhat battered image at the level of international amateur competition.

Actually, the first National Team to appear in world tournaments was the old Winnipeg Maroons, who won the Allan Cup in 1964. However, in the public mind, the National Team is the group of young students who were assembled by Father David Bauer at the University of British Columbia in the autumn of 1962. The Maroons and Father Bauer's group amalgamated in September, 1965, at Winnipeg, which became headquarters for the combined project.

The dream still persists today, surviving many vicissitudes. The National Team received a death sentence in January, 1970, when Canada withdrew from international hockey competition. But the dream didn't die. The National Team was given a new lease on life when it was revived to represent Canada in the Olympic Games of 1980, 1984 and 1988.

The spiritual leader of the National Team concept has always been Father David Bauer, a Basilian priest. Father Bauer came by his hockey credentials honestly. One of his older brothers, Bobby Bauer, partnered Milt Schmidt and Woody Dumart on the famous "Kraut Line" of the Boston Bruins.

David Bauer also was a good hockey player. He was a centre and left-winger on some outstanding junior teams at St. Michael's College in Toronto. And, in 1943, the Oshawa Generals induced him to play for them in the Memorial Cup finals when they won the Canadian junior championship, defeating Trail, B.C.

A year of army service interrupted his education at St. Michael's. After-wards, he attended the University of Toronto for a year before entering the Basilian Seminary. Ordained to the priesthood, he was assigned to the teaching staff of St. Michael's College, where he coached hockey from 1954 through 1961.

Father Bauer gained a formidable reputation as a motivator and coach at St. Michael's. In 1961, his final year at the college, his team won the junior championship of Canada. They defeated the Edmonton Oil Kings, four games to two, in the Memorial Cup series.

Bauer had some fine hockey players on his 1961 roster. His two goalies, Gerry Cheevers and Dave Dryden, became distinguished professionals. Other members of the team who ultimately played in the NHL were Rod Seiling, Billy MacMillan, Arnie Brown, Larry Keenan, Terry Clancy and Barry MacKenzie.

Opposite: St. Michael's College hockey team, 1934. *Public Archives Canada/PA 49523* **Above: Father David Bauer coached the St. Michael's College hockey team from 1954 to 1961.** *Hockey Hall of Fame*

One man who didn't turn pro was Terry O'Malley. However, he did play for the National Team as early as 1962 and was still playing for them in the 1980 Olympics.

After that Memorial Cup victory, Father Bauer's superiors assigned him to St. Mark's College, an affiliate of the University of British Columbia.

Meanwhile, the operators of the Canadian Amateur Hockey Association were becoming increasingly disturbed by the evidence that Canada was losing ground internationally. The Galt Terriers had failed to win the world tournament at Colorado Springs in 1962, despite the fact that two major European powers, the Soviet Union and Czechoslovakia, weren't represented. Sweden won the championship with a 5-3 victory over Canada. In that sorry context, the CAHA was forced to acknowledge that our Allan Cup champions no longer could be expected to win in the international arena.

Coincidentally, one of Father Bauer's older brothers, Ray Bauer, had persuaded the priest to travel to Colorado Springs to observe for himself how Canada was falling behind the Europeans. Ray Bauer had been one of the financial backers of the Kitchener-Waterloo Dutchmen, who failed to win the gold medals at the Olympics of 1956 and 1960. The Dutchmen finished third in 1956 and they were second in 1960.

In Colorado Springs, Father Bauer had some exhaustive conversations with CAHA president Jack Roxborough and executive director Gordon Jukes. The consensus of opinion was that Canada must embark on a radical new course, even going to the extent of establishing a permanent team composed largely of university students, supplemented by the best available senior amateur players. There was agreement in principle that such a team must have a permanent training base and that it should play a full schedule of games against minor league professional teams. Roxborough asked Father Bauer to produce a written plan and submit it to the annual meeting of the CAHA at the Westbury Hotel in Toronto in June, 1962.

All provincial branches of the CAHA were represented at that 1962 meeting, and they unanimously endorsed the concept of a national team. Some preliminary funding was provided, and Father Bauer was empowered to select a group of suitable hockey-playing students and to get them enrolled at the University of British Columbia.

When Father Bauer first arrived at St. Mark's College, UBC was bursting at the seams, in the throes of a vast expansion program which made it one of the largest universities in Canada. The university's hockey program was in a state of flux. There were only two ice-arenas in Vancouver. The Forum was the home of the professional Vancouver Canucks. The other rink was the Kerrisdale Arena. The university hockey team was fortunate to get three practices per week in the Kerrisdale Arena — two at night and the other at noon on Thursdays.

In these unpropitious circumstances, Father Bauer began to assemble his first team. The initial batch of recruits who enrolled at UBC included Terry O'Malley and Barry MacKenzie from his 1961 Memorial Cup championship team, goalie Ken Broderick, and Dave Chambers. The latter became a successful college coach, who later coached the Italian National Team at the 1982 world tournament in Helsinki, Finland.

In 1987, Bauer recalled those early days: "We didn't have a rink. The student drive to build one on the campus was just getting underway. We didn't have a full quota of players; we didn't have uniforms or sticks — and we didn't have money."

Actually, some money was available, but it didn't last long. Emulating his older and revered fellow-priest, Monsignor Athol Murray, the founder of Notre Dame College in Wilcox, Saskatchewan, Father Bauer convinced some of his family friends back in Kitchener that the National Team was a worthy cause. Even his mother, Mrs. Edgar Bauer, contributed a gift of several thousand dollars to keep things going in Vancouver.

The players themselves proved to be remarkably adaptable. Barry MacKenzie discovered that a bus manufacturer in Toronto wanted to have a bus delivered to a customer in Edmonton. MacKenzie loaded a dozen aspiring young hockey players into the bus and, bolstered by the $75 that the manufacturer had given him for gasoline money, they went to Edmonton. After all, Edmonton was three-quarters of the way to Vancouver.

The CAHA had provided the players with money to cover their university fees, plus a very modest allowance for food and lodgings. Cheerfully, they pitched in to become the most ingenious scroungers in the history of any Canadian hockey enterprise.

Right in the middle of the UBC campus, they discovered an abandoned house, which had been used as a traffic-control office. They laid claim to this old wreck. Then one of Father Bauer's mysterious benefactors provided a prefabricated unit, which volunteer carpenters attached to the original house. Soon all the hockey players were lodged in their own makeshift dormitory. They next hired a woman who, for a modest fee, was happy to cook meals for them.

To furnish their quarters, the hockey players picked up almost anything that wasn't nailed down. Terry O'Malley recalls meeting Marshall Johnston walking across the campus one dark night. Johnston was carrying two chairs on his back. As they met, Johnston said cryptically, "Don't ask any silly questions."

By the early autumn of 1964, 18 hockey players were living in the makeshift quarters when Father Bauer persuaded Andy O'Brien, the Montreal newspaperman to pay a visit. O'Brien was sports editor of *Weekend Magazine*, which was circulated nationally as a supplement to major daily newspapers, all the way from Newfoundland to Victoria. *Weekend* had, by far, the largest circulation of any magazine in Canada.

When he returned to Montreal, O'Brien assigned William McCarthy to write a story about the manner in which the financially strapped members of the National Team were coping with their problems out on the Pacific Coast. McCarthy's article brought a great deal of attention to the National Team; a large number of Canadians responded emotionally and materially.

Much more importantly, O'Brien was a member of the Fitness Council,

A visit by the 1964-65 National Team to the Canadian NORAD base in Germany.
T. O'Malley

which was financed by the federal government. At the next meeting of the Fitness Council, O'Brien, whose Irish eloquence was quite impressive, had his fellow-councillors sobbing in their seats as he told them of the Spartan living conditions of the young hockey players on the UBC campus. The members thereupon voted unanimously to make a cash grant of $25,000 to the National Team. It was the first really impressive chunk of money to be bestowed upon the infant enterprise.

The National Team had been established by the CAHA for the immediate purpose of representing Canada in the Olympic Games of 1964. However, in the building process, Father Bauer experienced tremendous difficulty in arranging anything resembling a sensible schedule of games. In their rookie season, they engaged in exhibition matches with Portland, Seattle and Vancouver of the Western Hockey League. They'd play against any senior or junior team willing to accommodate them. Occasionally, they went as long as three weeks without playing a game.

The highlight of that initial season was a series of matches with the touring Czech National Team. They went east to play games against the Czechs in

Sudbury and Winnipeg. The climax of the tour was a home-game against the Czechs in the Vancouver Forum, which the Canadians won.

Using college players was still a basic concept of the National Team, coming up to the 1964 Olympics, which would be staged at Innsbruck, Austria. However, realizing that the competition at Innsbruck would be considerably better than anything they had encountered in the 18 months of preparation for their first major test, Father Bauer asked for some reinforcements.

The first addition was Seth Martin. He was, in all probability, the best goaltender outside the six-team NHL at that time. Martin had played for the Trail Smoke-Eaters, who, in 1961, had been the last Canadian team to win one of those world championship tournaments in Europe. Other notable recruits were Brian Conacher, Roger Bourbonnais (former captain of the Edmonton Oil Kings) and Rod Seiling. The latter, who was destined to play in the NHL for 16 seasons, had been loaned to the National Team by the Toronto Marlboros.

In their first exposure to the top grade of international competition — and, incidentally, their first exposure to the machinations of "Bunny" Ahearne and his IIHF satraps — the young Canadians performed very creditably. They lost only two games at Innsbruck. The Czechs defeated them, 3-1, and the Soviets had difficulty in subduing them, 3-2.

The Soviet Union dominated the tournament with seven victories and no defeats. Three countries — Canada, Sweden and Czechoslovakia — finished with identical records: five wins and two losses. On the final day of the tournament, Father Bauer and his players were instructed to report to the Innsbruck Arena for the medal presentation ceremonies. The Canadians fully expected to receive the bronze medals because they had beaten Sweden, 3-1. But when the presentations were made, Sweden received the second-place silver medals and the Czechs received the third-place bronzes.

The Canadians were stunned. They couldn't believe that the IIHF tie-breaking formula, which had been improvised only a few minutes before the official presentation, would drop them all the way to fourth place in the tournament. Father Bauer attempted to placate his bitterly disillusioned young players by telling them that this was a "learning experience." Marshall Johnston broke the tension at the Canadian team's post-mortem meeting. He stood in the centre of the room, raised his hands for silence and said to Bauer, "Father, your flock was fleeced."

After the 1964 Olympics, Winnipeg became the permanent headquarters of the National Team. Although he was still the leader of the operation, Father Bauer abandoned his active coaching role. He remained on the staff at St. Mark's in Vancouver. Those players who were taking courses at the University of British Columbia shifted to the University of Manitoba and associated colleges in Winnipeg.

Gordon Simpson took over the coaching of the National Team for the 1965 season but, soon thereafter, relinquished the job to Jackie McLeod of Saskatoon, who had played for the New York Rangers in the NHL. McLeod had considerable experience in international hockey. He had travelled to European tournaments with the Trail Smoke-Eaters and the Saskatoon Quakers.

Geographically, Winnipeg, right in the middle of Canada, was an ideal location for a team that was drawing its players from all sections of the country. Another prime consideration in the selection of Winnipeg was the fact that the National Team could play a full schedule of games with the minor professional teams of the Central Hockey League in the United States.

The clubs of the National Hockey League, privately, were completely and unalterably opposed to Father Bauer's operation. They did everything in their power to deter promising young players from involvement in the National Team program. The NHL's selfishness was understandable: the league was planning to double in size in 1967 — expanding from six clubs to twelve — and they needed every available young player to stock those six new teams.

Until the federal government coerced the Toronto Maple Leafs and the Montreal Canadiens into joining the newly formed Hockey Canada organization in 1969, those two clubs looked upon Father Bauer as a dangerous enemy.

The late Clarence S. Campbell, president of the National Hockey League, usually was the epitome of reasonableness. He was always capable of seeing the other man's side in an argument. But there was a time when Campbell became almost paranoid on the subject of Father Bauer. His paranoia was shared by all NHL club-owners, one of whom, to his everlasting discredit, was reported to have said that Bauer "really is a hockey-man, who just moonlights in the priesthood."

Typical of the NHL attempts to frustrate the Bauer program was the case of Serge Savard, a junior defenceman. His parents had signed one of those documents, known as "C forms," which committed Serge to join the Montreal Canadiens, if and when he turned professional. The Canadiens weren't in any hurry for Savard's services until one morning they heard that the young defenceman was on his way to Dorval Airport, where he would board a plane for the Winnipeg headquarters of the National Team. Quickly, Sammy Pollock, general manager of the Canadiens, dispatched an agent to Dorval Airport with instructions to grab Savard and bring him back to the Montreal Forum. Savard, who would have been of tremendous assistance to the National Team, stayed in Montreal when Pollock gave him a commitment that, within a year, he'd get his chance to play for Les Canadiens in the NHL.

Pollock's attitude changed dramatically after the Canadiens became involved in Hockey Canada. Not only did Sam become a supporter of the National Team program, but he has also been the chairman of Hockey Canada's International Committee since 1980.

When Father Bauer and Coach Jack McLeod took their team into Ljubljana, Yugoslavia, for the world tournament of 1966, they were blissfully unaware that their young club was in danger of being blown apart, permanently, by frustration.

To put things into perspective, it should be explained that the Canadians finished third in that Yugoslavian tournament. They defeated the Swedes, the Americans, the Poles, the Finns and the West Germans. They lost only to the Soviets and the Czechoslovakians. It was in their game against the Czechs, on March 10, 1966, that the balloon went up.

The Canadians actually scored three goals, but the referees, Andrei Choj-nacki of Poland and Genaro Olicieri of Switzerland, nullified two of those goals.

The 1966 National Team in a game against the Soviets.
Dan Diamond

Accordingly, the official result of the game was Czechoslovakia 2, Canada 1.

There can be no question that the Canadians were robbed by the referees. This wasn't merely another case of Canadians whimpering that the officials were stupid; even the international press united in agreement that Canada had been fleeced. The following day, *Politik Belgrade* headlined its hockey story: "Referees Rob Canada of Victory." *Vecernje Novosti* of Belgrade proclaimed: "Referees Against Canada." *Borba* of Belgrade headed its story: "Referees Decide Top of Standing."

Borba reported: "The referees gave unjust decisions. . . . In the first serious game for the Medals, the so-called representatives of justice began to shape the standings. . . . The Canadians did not lose this match — the two points were taken away from them. Czech goalie Vladimir Dzurilla was in fact beaten three times but he, in contrast with Seth Martin of Canada, had behind him the referees who defended the Czechoslovakian net better than Dzurilla."

Sportske Novosti, the Belgrade sports paper, described the officiating as "shameful." The paper went on to say that the 11 penalties imposed on Canada (compared with only three against the Czechs) left Father Bauer "pale and shaken."

Father Bauer had to face an incipient mutiny when he went into the dressing room after that game. The players were in such a fury that they voted informally to quit the tournament right there. They would go home without playing their final game against the Russians.

The debate raged in the dressing room all night. Bauer argued that the players would be making a fatal mistake by quitting the tournament. He pointed out that, in the previous 12 months, the Canadian news media and the Canadian public finally had united in support of the National Team. If they quit now, Bauer argued, they would be hammered by the Canadian press and public who would dump on them as "quitters" and "crybabies."

The priest's eloquence was not enough, initially. In this emergency, Bauer importuned two Canadian newspaper friends, Jim Proudfoot of the *Toronto Star* and George Gross of the *Toronto Telegram*. Bauer asked the newspapermen to go into the dressing room and explain the facts of life to the hockey players. He was confident that Proudfoot and Gross would tell the players that they would be certain to alienate the newly supportive Canadian public if, in this fit of anger, they pulled out of the world tournament.

Father Bauer was appalled by what happened next. Proudfoot and Gross, after listening to the beefs of the outraged players for half an hour, stood up in the middle of the dressing room and said, in effect: "You're right! You've been treated shamefully! You should stalk out of here, right now, and board the first available plane for Canada!"

A lesser man might have surrendered, but Father Bauer wasn't finished. After the newspapermen failed him, he went out and induced a senior Canadian diplomat to address the players. Apparently, the diplomat was persuasive because, very reluctantly, they agreed to stay.

It was approximately 5 A.M. before the players resolved their own fate. Then, with little or no sleep, they went out the following afternoon and lost to the Soviets, 3-0.

At the very least, they had honoured their commitments to the tournament. Coach McLeod put it another way. He said bitterly, "We should have quit. We stayed for only one reason — Father Dave!"

Despite Father Bauer's misgivings, the members of the team were national heroes when they returned to Canada. The Canadian public shared their outrage over the officiating in Ljubljana. For the first time, the nation had been aroused, from coast to coast, and had taken the hockey players to their hearts.

Adulation for the National Team reached an all-time peak slightly more than nine months after the debacle of Ljubljana. Canada's Centennial was to be celebrated in 1967, and the CAHA decided that the year should begin, suitably, with a Centennial invitational hockey tournament in Winnipeg. The Soviet Union, Czechoslovakia and the United States were invited to send teams.

Emotionally, it was an amazingly gratifying enterprise, not only for the hockey team, but also for the citizens of Winnipeg. For that first week in January, Winnipeg was the hub of interest for Canadians across the country as they watched the games telecast from the Winnipeg Arena on national television. Winnipeggers gloried in their exposure in the national spotlight, and the National Team provided the most rewarding performance in its entire history.

Before record crowds in the Winnipeg Arena, Canada responded to the wild fan support by defeating the Americans and the Czechs. Then, while every sports fanatic in the country waited tensely, the final match against the Soviets was set up for the night of Friday, January 8, 1967. It mattered not a whit to Canadians that the Czechs had beaten Russia, 5-2, in a preliminary match. This was to be the game everyone had been waiting for — Canada versus the Soviets — on our own ground!

A record Winnipeg crowd of 10,442, including Prime Minister Lester B. Pearson, jammed the arena for the tournament finale. To the distress of their admirers — in the arena as well as in the vast television audience — things didn't go well for the Canadians in the early stages. They fell behind, 1-3, before they hit their true stride in the second period.

Carl Brewer, a recent addition to the team after quitting the Toronto Maple Leafs, scored Canada's second goal at 8:07 of that second period. Jean Cusson tied the score at 12:44, and then Gary Dineen gave Canada a 4-3 lead at 18:51 after Cusson's forechecking had set up the scoring play.

However, the Soviets weren't finished. Early in the third period, Paramoshkin capitalized on a power play to deadlock the game at 4-4. It remained for Billy MacMillan to score the winning goal, only 14 seconds after Paramoshkin had beaten Canada's 21-year-old goalie, Wayne Stephenson.

The national euphoria should have been tempered by the fact that, obviously, the Soviets hadn't sent their best players to the Centennial tournament. In fact, Russia's most successful coach, Anatoli Tarasov, had remained at home, and he had delegated his chores to his longtime associate, Arkady Chernyshev. For his part, Chernyshev had benched four of his players on the eve of the game against Canada. He was displeased by their performance in the loss to Czechoslovakia. Chernyshev, always gentlemanly, congratulated the Canadians but, with a quiet smile, he warned that there might be "a different story" at the 1967 world tournament at Vienna in April.

Many survivors of The Noble Experiment are of the opinion that the National Team was at its peak in 1967, when the defence was anchored by Carl Brewer and Jack Bownass. Early in 1967, a second branch of the National Team had been set up in Ottawa. Bownass, a reinstated amateur with lengthy professional experience, became playing-coach of that Ottawa group. Brewer was one of the better professional defencemen of his generation. He had been selected for the NHL First All-Star Team in the 1962-63 season. In two other seasons, he was selected for the Second All-Star Team.

Although Brewer was a highly talented player, he had a mind of his own and he had a personality conflict with "Punch" Imlach, the sometimes dictatorial manager-coach of the Toronto Maple Leafs. The upshot of their quibbling was that Brewer — saying that he'd like to join Father Bauer's project — declined to report to the Toronto training camp in the autumn of 1966. Imlach, a man who refused to coddle recalcitrant employees, convinced the Maple Leaf club-owners that they should permit Brewer to have his amateur reinstatement. That became a big plus for the National Team, and Brewer's absence didn't affect the Maple Leafs deleteriously. Without him, they won the Stanley Cup in May, 1967.

The Canadians left with high hopes for the 1967 world tournament in Vienna. But Arkady Chernyshev hadn't been jesting when he predicted that the Soviets would be an improved team in Austria. The Russians swept through the tournament, winning all seven games on their schedule. In the final game, they defeated Canada, 2-1. Moreover, the Canadians had blown their chances earlier in the week. They were caught napping by the Swedes, who gave them a 6-0 shellacking.

Then, in their final game of the tournament, against the Czechs, the Canadians discovered that European officiating hadn't improved significantly in the year since they had been victimized at Ljubljana. The referee in this case was Ove Dahlberg of Sweden. Videotapes of that game confirmed that Dahlberg must have been suffering from acute myopia.

The official score was Canada 1, Czechoslovakia 1. However, Billy MacMillan scored what should have proved to be the winning goal for Canada, only to have that goal disallowed by Dahlberg. Dahlberg ruled that Jean Cusson had been inside the Czech goaltending crease when MacMillan shot the puck into the net.

Later, the films and videotapes of the incident were made available to Canadian officials at the tournament. Those films and tapes showed clearly that Cusson had been five feet away from the goaltending crease when MacMillan fired the scoring shot. There was no point in protesting after the cattle had been stolen from the barn. Canada, which finished with a record identical to Sweden's — four wins, two losses and one tie — settled for the bronze medals. That 1967 team may have been, as the former players now say, the best squad assembled during the Father Bauer regime. However, apart from that Winnipeg Centennial tournament win, it didn't manage to win the Big Ones.

Today, Father Bauer probably would concede that his major goal was victory in the Olympic Games. Philosophically, at least, the Games epitomized the highest ideals of genuinely amateur sport. The 1964 Olympics had been rather disillusioning for the young players, and the 1968 Olympics at Grenoble, France, were to fall short of Bauer's fondest hopes.

At Grenoble, the Canadians stumbled in their second game when they took a completely unexpected 5-2 beating from Finland. The only other teams that the Finns managed to defeat at Grenoble were West Germany and East Germany. The National Team was knocked offstride by that defeat. They didn't begin to regain their top form until they came up against Czechoslovakia. That year's Czech team was outstanding. In the 1968 tournament, they were the only team able to defeat the Soviets. However, against the Czechs, the Canadians played their best hockey in two weeks. They won, 3-2, after protecting their one-goal lead desperately in a tense third period.

So, after riding an emotional roller-coaster, the Canadians came into the final day of the tournament with an opportunity to win the gold medals, if they could defeat the Soviets. Their game against the Russians was a distinct disappointment. Canada had a power-play advantage, early, and they messed it up. Gary Dineen took too much time getting to a loose puck in the middle-ice zone. Beating Dineen to that loose puck, Anatoli Firsov skated in and scored easily. The Soviets went on to a 5-0 victory.

The National Team's two trips to the Olympics had achieved modest results.

Canada's Marshall Johnston (right) scores with an assist from Terry O'Malley (left) during the United States vs. Canada Olympic hockey game in Grenoble, France, February 11, 1968. *Canapress*

They were cheated out of medals in 1964, and they had to settle for the bronze medals in 1968.

Our recurring failures on the international scene weren't being accepted graciously by the Canadian public. The hard, sobering facts were that we hadn't won an Olympic championship since 1952, and seven years had passed since the Trail Smoke-Eaters last won one of those world championships on European ice. Members of the federal government were being made keenly aware of public lamentations that European nations were beating us consistently in our national sport.

In December, 1968, the federal government finally acted very forcefully by sponsoring the creation of an umbrella organization, named Hockey Canada. Under the leadership of John Munro, minister of health and welfare, Hockey Canada was empowered to consolidate the efforts of Canada's many divergent hockey enterprises into one national program. The groups designated for membership in this organization included: Canada's two NHL clubs, the

Toronto Maple Leafs and the Montreal Canadiens; the Canadian Amateur Hockey Association; and the NHL Players' Association.

The formation of Hockey Canada assured Father Bauer's National Team of being bankrolled comfortably with federal government funds, although things were moving swiftly towards a schism in the international hockey world.

The National Team's first trip abroad under the aegis of Hockey Canada was for the 1969 world tournament in Stockholm, Sweden. It was a team in transition — many new young players were being introduced to the lineup — and the results in Stockholm were less than satisfactory.

Canada played ten games at Stockholm and lost six of them. They lost two games to the champion Czechs, two to the Soviets and two to the saintly Swedes. Canada's only wins were scored at the expense of the Americans and the Finns.

The Stockholm tournament can be remembered chiefly for the fact that it marked the debut on the international scene of two notable Canadians: goalie Ken Dryden and Alan Eagleson. Dryden had just completed his final examinations at Cornell University and, when goalie Steve Rexe obligingly sustained a "knee injury," Dryden was flown to Stockholm as an emergency replacement. The purpose of Eagleson's visit was fairly obvious. Hockey Canada already was working towards the admission of Canada's professional players to international tournaments. Before leaving Toronto, Eagleson told reporters that the first item on his agenda was to seek a meeting with "Bunny" Ahearne, president of the IIHF.

When he was advised of Eagleson's impending arrival, Ahearne retorted snootily that he wasn't about to grant an audience to "a messenger-boy for a trades union." Nevertheless, pressure from his IIHF colleagues impelled Ahearne to meet Eagleson one afternoon in a room at Stockholm's Grand Hotel. Jim Proudfoot of the *Toronto Star* and I were waiting for Eagleson in the Grand Hotel bar after he emerged from his session with "Bunny." Eagleson had been talking so earnestly that he required two full tumblers of ice-cold orange juice to cool his vocal cords.

The fact that the federal government was taking a very active interest in hockey was not lost on the European members of the IIHF, even if Ahearne professed to be profoundly unimpressed. Already, the IIHF had awarded the 1970 world tournament to Canada — the first time it would be played in our country. The games were scheduled to be split between the Winnipeg Arena and the Montreal Forum. Then, at the IIHF meeting in Crans, Switzerland, in the early summer of 1969, there was another rather surprising concession. The delegates agreed that, in all future world competitions, Canada would be permitted to use nine minor league professionals, plus reinstated amateurs. In plain language, this meant that the National Team could be bolstered by nine players of American Hockey League calibre.

Ironically, the events of the next eight months would suggest that this decision at Crans — which was viewed by Canadians as an important breakthrough — may have hastened the demise of the National Team.

An invitational tournament in Leningrad was scheduled for the autumn of 1969. Wishing to assess any improvements that could be gained from the new

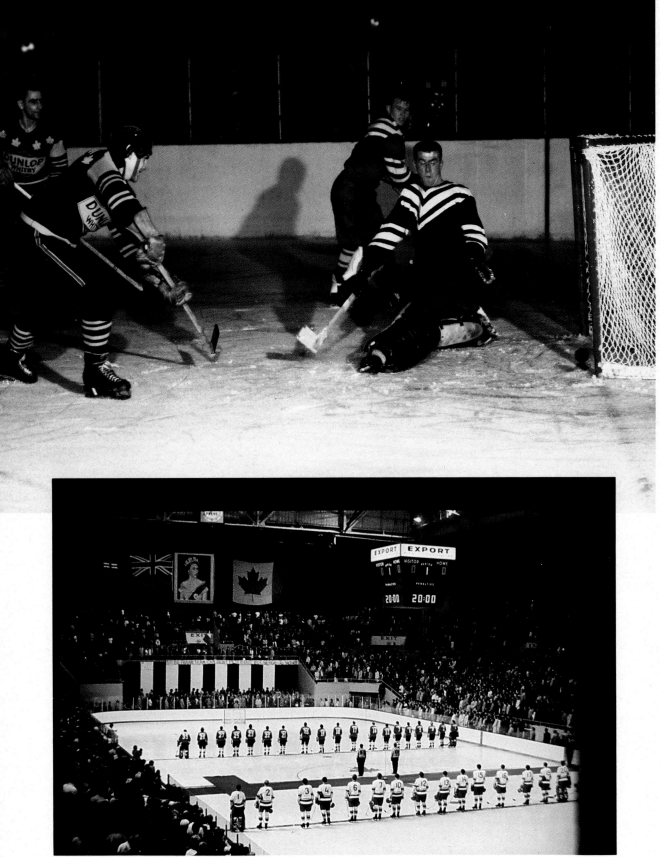

Top: The Whitby Dunlops, winners of the 1958 world championship. *Hockey Hall of Fame*
Bottom: The 1972 Summit Series' Opening Ceremonies of Game Three. *Brian Pickell*

Ron Ellis checked by Gennadiy Tsigankov. *Brian Pickell*

Paul Henderson. *Brian Pickell*

Harry Sinden, Team Canada coach. *Brian Pickell*

Yvan Cournoyer scores in the third period of Game Two to put Canada two goals ahead. *Brian Pickell*

Overleaf: Some of the 2,700 Canadians who travelled to Moscow with Team Canada. *Brian Pickell*

Jean-Paul Parise checks Alexander Maltsev. *Brian Pickell*

Paul Henderson is carried on the shoulders of Phil Esposito and Alan Eagleson in Toronto's Nathan Phillips Square. *Brian Pickell*

Phil Esposito after the winning goal of the series. *Brian Pickell*

Darryl Sittler, 1976 Canada Cup. *James Lipa*

Alexander Maltsev, 1976 Canada Cup. *James Lipa*

Top: 1981 Canada Cup. *James Lipa* **Bottom: John Tonelli, 1984 Canada Cup.** *James Lipa*

Left: Guy Lafleur, 1981 Canada Cup. *James Lipa*
Below: 1976 Canada Cup. *James Lipa*

Wayne Gretzky vs. Valeriy Vasiliev, 1984 Canada Cup. *James Lipa*

Wayne Gretzky, 1984 Canada Cup. *James Lipa*

1984 Olympics. *James Lipa*

1985 world championship game in Prague. *James Lipa*

eligibility rules, the National Team added the following group of players: Guy Lapointe, Al MacNeil, Phil Roberto, Jim McKenney, Wayne Carleton, Jean Gauthier, Chuck Hamilton, Gary Marsh, Danny Johnson and André Hense. A few years later, Lapointe would be an NHL All-Star defenceman. MacNeil would coach the Montreal Canadiens to a Stanley Cup victory. Jimmy McKenney became a longtime Toronto Maple Leaf — highly talented but remembered best as the Toronto club's resident jester.

Regrettably, the Canadians played just a bit too well at Leningrad. They finished second in the tournament. The Soviets, particularly, had a distinct change of heart about permitting Canada to use professionals. They found a ready ally in Ahearne, who always had been opposed to Canada's use of professionals. The Czechs, other Iron Curtain countries and Sweden fell into line behind the Soviets.

Canada was targeted for an historic double-cross when the IIHF next convened at Geneva on January 4, 1970. The Europeans crassly repudiated their previous agreement to permit Canada to use nine minor league professionals. Ahearne provided an ingenious excuse for their action. He reported that the International Olympic Committee would be forced to bar the Soviets, Czechs, Swedes and other countries from the 1972 Olympic Games if they played in any hockey matches against the Canadian professionals. It was, of course, hogwash! But the Soviets and their satellites voted against Canada without even the slightest blush of shame. Knowing that the federal government would back them to the hilt, the Canadian delegation promptly pulled their country out of any further international hockey tournaments.

Back home, the news stunned the members of the National Team, just as they were preparing to go onto the Ottawa Auditorium ice for an exhibition game with the touring Czechoslovakians. Canada's decision was irrevocable and it could mean only one thing: the National Team was out of business.

The repercussions were loud and long-lasting. Everywhere in Canada — with the very particular exception of Winnipeg — Canadians applauded the actions of our hockey delegates in Crans. The nation was fed up with European double-dealings. The consensus of Canadian opinion was: "To hell with them! They've shoved us around once too often!"

At the same time, everyone sympathized with the plight of the players on the National Team. It soon became obvious that, with no more international competitions available, the Nationals had become an expensive luxury for the federal government. The team scarcely could be expected to generate gate-receipts from meaningless exhibition games with teams in Canada. The reason for the National Team's existence had disappeared with Canada's decision to stay out of international competition.

Winnipeggers, for their part, were outraged. Canada's withdrawal meant that the 1970 world tournament was kaput. (Eventually, it was awarded to Sweden.) Remarkably, Montreal, which had been assigned to split the tournament games with Winnipeg, reacted with a yawn. Les Canadiens were the hockey attraction in La Belle Province, and Montrealers didn't feel upset by the loss of another opportunity to watch the touring Soviets, Czechs and Swedes.

Winnipeggers, however, felt betrayed. The city had become the permanent home of the National Team. Western Canadian philanthropists had banded together to build a permanent training facility for the Nats — an arena at St. John's-Ravenscourt, a private school in Winnipeg. But what Winnipeggers resented most was the lost efforts they already had made to sell out their arena for the 1970 tournament. They were also boiling with indignation because their city had lost its opportunity to occupy, for a few ego-nourishing days, the spotlight at centre stage in the international sporting arena.

Knowing that their actions had the full support of the federal government, the governors of Hockey Canada hunkered down and made the best of an unfortunate situation. Unequivocally, they honoured all their financial obligations to members of the National Team who had enrolled in university courses. Most of those players stayed in college until they obtained degrees.

In that 1962-70 era, when it is remembered as "Father Bauer's Team," 83 players went through the National Team system.

In addition to the pioneering Seth Martin, there were two other National Team goalies who became famous. Wayne Stephenson later played for the Philadelphia Flyers when they won the Stanley Cup. Ken Dryden, probably the most distinguished of all National Team graduates, was voted into the Hockey Hall of Fame in 1983. Dryden studied law at the University of Manitoba while he was playing for the Nats, and he completed his studies at McGill on a Hockey Canada scholarship after he turned professional.

Some of the other players who went into the NHL after having National Team experience were Bob Berry, "Butch" Goring, Marshall Johnston, Brian Glennie, Ab DeMarco, Chuck Lefley, Danny O'Shea, Kevin O'Shea, Gerry Pinder, Billy MacMillan, Bob Murdoch and Fran Huck. Berry, Goring, Johnston, Murdoch and MacMillan all became head coaches in the NHL.

Left: Bob Berry, a National Team graduate who made a career of coaching hockey. *Hockey Hall of Fame* **Centre: Butch Goring played in the NHL and on Team Canada before becoming a head coach.** *James Lipa*

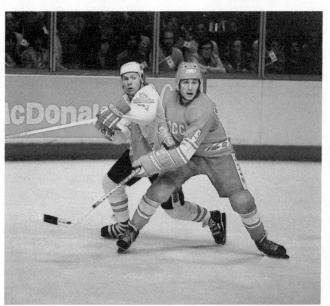

More importantly, the National Team experiment produced some remarkable individuals who demonstrated the inherent wisdom of combining a university education with a career in international sports. Ken Dryden, Roger Bourbonnais, Gary Begg, Fran Huck and Herb Pinder all graduated from law school. Morris Mott became a professor of history. Barry MacKenzie and Terry O'Malley became school teachers. MacKenzie now is principal of Notre Dame College in Wilcox, Saskatchewan. Huck, after practicing law, returned to the same college as an administrator.

Four members of "the original cast" still are working within shouting distance of one another on the campus of the University of British Columbia. Bob Hindmarch, who managed the pioneering National Team squad, is director of sports services and athletics at U.B.C. Father Bauer is still on the staff of St. Mark's College and, as a governor of Hockey Canada, he is involved deeply in the Olympic Hockey Program. Terry O'Malley, who followed Father Bauer to Vancouver in 1962, has returned to U.B.C. as coach of the hockey team. Rick Noonan, who has been associated with Father Bauer since his schooldays at St. Michael's in Toronto, is director of men's athletics at the university.

Among the Canadian news media, Noonan has a reputation for popping up at international hockey events. He was a trainer for the National Team in its final years. When Canada returned to world championship competitions at Vienna in 1977, Noonan was the team's trainer. He was general manager of Canada's Olympic Team at Lake Placid in 1980.

In September 1972, Canadian reporters went to the Montreal Forum to watch Team Soviet's final practice before the opening of the famous Summit Series. Glancing at the sweater-clad men working behind the Soviet bench, the reporters spotted a familiar face. Sure enough, it was Rick Noonan — working for the Russians! Noonan was working for Team Soviet, but he was being paid by Hockey Canada.

On instructions from Chris Lang of Hockey Canada, Noonan devoted himself 24 hours per day to the service of the Soviets. He helped them with their equipment, and he assisted with loading all their luggage in and out of airplanes and hotels throughout their entire stay in Canada. Unfortunately, he was unable to pick up any Soviet hockey secrets in their dressing room. Noonan spoke no Russian, and the Soviets stuck to their native tongue. However, the players kept him busy with their demands for hot tea. Georgio, the Soviet trainer, had other requests; he expected Noonan to keep him supplied with vodka and Canadian rye whiskey.

"I worked for them from the time they arrived in Toronto until they flew home from Vancouver," Noonan says now. "We seemed to get along okay, but they didn't invite me to go back to Moscow with them. And all the time they were in Canada, I felt a bit like a pariah because my Canadian media-buddies kept telling me that they suspected me of being a traitor."

Fifteen years after Father Bauer put together his first young squad, a strong spirit of camaraderie still is evident among the individuals who had any part in the project. The formation of the National Team was a magnificent concept. The many men who were involved in it brought honour to their country and to themselves.

Below: Marshall Johnston became a head coach in the NHL. *James Lipa* Overleaf: National Team graduate Ken Dryden in action as Team Canada '72's goaltender. *Canapress*

PATTINSON TROPHY   ALLAN CUP   SCOTLAND WOOLEN
MANITOBA   MILLS TROPHY
CHAMPIONSHIP   THUNDER BAY
                                   CHAMPIONSHIP

PORT ARTHUR HOCKEY TEAM
WINNERS OF ALLAN CUP 1929

Vair Price Cox Friday Creighton Gross Baker Wilson L'Heureux Jarvis Barton McC

Top: The Victoria Hockey Team, Winnipeg, world champions 1894–95. Public Archives Canada/PA 50669
Bottom: The Port Arthur Bearcats represented Canada at the 1930 world championship.
Public Archives Canada/PA 49603

5 WORLD CHAMPIONSHIP TOURNAMENTS

THE WORLD CHAMPIONSHIPS WERE INVENTED BY THE EUROPEANS, who controlled the International Ice Hockey Federation. Canadians, smugly confident that the best hockey in the universe was played in the North American professional leagues, usually managed to ignore the earliest world tournaments, which were played in Europe. We didn't take those championships very seriously until the Soviets made their first appearance in 1954. There was no complacency left in this country after the shockwaves, emanating from Stockholm, rattled the very foundations of the Canadian sports structure.

Initially, the IIHF had decreed that the Olympic champions also should be recognized as world champions. In that format, Canada automatically won the world championship in 1920, 1924, 1928 and 1932. In 1930, the IIHF decided to stage world championships in non-Olympic years. The 1930 tournament was awarded to Berlin, and the CAHA gave the Port Arthur Bearcats the right to represent Canada. The Bearcats had won the Allan Cup the previous year.

It is interesting to note that Japan was represented at that first world tourney. Artificial-ice arenas had been built in Japan in the early 1920s. The Japanese picked up the idea when some of their world-travelling businessmen saw hockey played on artificial ice in Vancouver and Victoria.

The meagre records of that first tournament suggest that Canada was given a bye — all the way to the championship game. Apparently, the Bearcats merely practiced while the other 11 countries fought it out. When the Germans emerged as the survivors of the elimination rounds, the Bearcats beat them, 6-1, for the championship.

In 1931, Canadian interest in the world championships was confined largely to my hometown of Winnipeg. Canada was represented at Krynica, Poland, by the University of Manitoba Grads. The players were holdovers from the University of Manitoba team which had won the Allan Cup in 1928.

The Grads took only eight players when they left Winnipeg on their 21-game tour. Andy Blair, who had been the heart of their 1928 national championship team, had turned professional with the Toronto Maple Leafs. Blake Watson, who had starred in 1928, was taking post-graduate studies in Vienna, and he joined the Grads when they arrived in Europe. The rest of the lineup was composed of goalie Art Puttee, Gordon MacKenzie, Ward McVey, Jack Pidcock, Guy "Weary" Williamson, George Hill, Sammy McCallum and Frank Morris. The last two were non-collegemen filling in for graduates who couldn't make the trip.

Cochran   W. Stewart

The Manitobans won the 1931 world tournament with a record of four wins and one tie. They were held to a scoreless draw by Sweden. Most memorably, they were the only team in history to go through a world tournament without yielding even one goal. Art Puttee, the goaltender who established that unparalleled record, afterwards became fire commissioner for the Province of Manitoba.

The University of Manitoba team of 1928 had three future doctors — Blake Watson, Gordon MacKenzie and Ward Turvey — in their lineup when they won the Allan Cup in 1928. Turvey didn't go to Europe in 1931 because he had opened a private practice. In 1987, two of those men were still practicing — Dr. Turvey in Vancouver and Dr. Watson as chief of gynecology at the major hospital in Glendale, California.

The next two years were chastening for the Canadian hockey establishment. First, the Winnipegs had their narrow escape in the 1932 Olympics. Then, in 1933, Canada lost a world tournament for the first time. The Americans won the gold medals, defeating Canada, 2-1.

The dubious distinction of being the manager of the first Canadian team ever to be beaten in one of these international shinny festivals belongs to Harold Ballard. Although Ballard has been pilloried by several unauthorized biographers, I don't recall reading much about the loss sustained by the Toronto Nationals at the 1933 world championships in Prague.

Before leaving home, the Toronto team had been known as the National Sea Fleas. This ghastly nickname stemmed from the fact that they represented the National Yacht Club of Toronto. The yacht club members were heavily involved in racing powerboats — little hydroplanes powered by large, noisy

outboard engines. These racing boats had been nicknamed Sea Fleas by Lou Marsh, a Toronto sports editor, who participated in the races.

The Sea Fleas weren't popular in Toronto. They committed the unpardonable sin of beating the widely beloved Toronto Marlboros in the 1932 amateur playoffs. In that situation, Ballard, who had a flair for controversy even when he was a comparatively young man, turned his back on his fellow-Torontonians and announced that the Nationals would move to Montreal to play their Allan Cup final series against Fort William.

I was attending McGill in Montreal at the time, and I persuaded the *Winnipeg Tribune* to permit me to "cover" the Allan Cup finals for my hometown paper. They paid me $5 per game and — looking back on it — I concede readily that I was overpaid. The Nationals beat Fort William, two-straight. It was then that I met Ballard for the first time, and even now I can remember the initial blast of his genial bluster.

The Nationals, who were a moderately good hockey team, were coached by Harry Watson. I don't recall any national uproar when they became the first Canadian team to lose in Europe. We were storing up our lamentations for 1936.

You may wonder why Canada bothered to send teams to those early world championships. Well, after the stock market crash of October, 1929, Canada wallowed in an economic depression, which continued almost to the outbreak of World War II in August, 1939. There was widespread unemployment, and many hockey players — all those beyond the boundaries of the few professional leagues — were fortunate if they had a wage-paying trade or an office job. Money was in short supply, and few people could afford holiday trips. In those circumstances, the members of a hockey team looked forward quite eagerly to an invitation to play in a world tournament. It was an opportunity to travel, to visit foreign countries, and all at the expense of someone else.

The travelling hockey players appeared to overlook the fact that they, themselves, generated the funds which underwrote their journeys. They didn't go merely to a world tournament — they were booked to play 20 or 30 exhibition games in Europe, before and after the world championships. The gate-receipts from those exhibition games paid for a lot of hotel rooms and meals.

Ironically, one man who benefited from these annual excursions was John Francis Ahearne. Not even his bitterest detractors could deny that "Bunny" was sharper than jail-house coffee. He had come to England as a youngster, and after a World War I career as an underage radio-operator in the Merchant Marine, he had settled in London. Even then, he could scent a loose one pound banknote at a range of 300 yards. Correctly anticipating a post-war upswing in worldwide tourism, he established a company known as Blue Ribbon Travel — and it was a winner.

Many CAHA officials have professed a distrust for "Bunny" bordering on detestation. Nevertheless, in some remarkable manner, he managed to become the official booking-agent for all Canadian hockey teams that went to Europe.

The Canadians weren't Ahearne's only hockey clients. By 1934, he had

ingratiated himself with the proprietors of the Eastern Arenas Union in the United States, a group which was headed by George Brown of the Boston Garden. This group had a loud voice in the councils of the U.S. Amateur Hockey Association and, not surprisingly, they steered their travel business to Ahearne.

Ahearne did rather well from these contacts. He arranged the European tours for the Canadian and American teams. And he received the customary travel agent's commissions for booking tourists on trains and buses and into hotels. He missed no angles; his sister operated a minor-league hotel in London and, merely as a coincidence, travelling hockey players often found themselves booked into that hostelry.

In any event, time proved that the defeat of the Toronto National Sea Fleas at Prague in 1933 didn't quench the enthusiasm of Canadian amateur hockey teams for foreign travel. In 1934, the Saskatoon Quakers went to Milan, Italy, and won all five games on their schedule, defeating the Americans, 2-1, in the final. In 1935, the Winnipeg Monarchs were designated to travel to Davos, Switzerland. The Monarchs swept all six games, and they defeated Switzerland, 4-2, in the championship match.

The defeat of the Canadians by their British "cousins" at the Olympics of 1936 aroused a new sense of wariness in the offices of the Canadian Amateur Hockey Association. For the next three years — right up to the outbreak of World War II — they were careful to select good amateur teams to play in the world championships.

The Saskatoon Quakers, winners of the 1934 world championship. *Hockey Hall of Fame*

The Kimberley Dynamiters, the 1937 world champions.
Hockey Hall of Fame

The Kimberley Dynamiters, who went to London in 1937, weren't taking any chances of being thwarted by a committee-room ruling. They played to an inexplicable 1-1 draw with France, but they mowed down the rest of their opponents, outscoring them 60 goals to 4. The Dynamiters avenged the Olympic loss of 1936 by blanking Britain, 3-0, in the tournament final.

In 1938, the Sudbury Wolves went to Prague. The Wolves weren't overpowering — the upstart Hungarians tied them, 1-1 — but they were good enough to go through the tournament without losing a game. They eliminated Germany from the semifinals, and they defeated Britain, 3-2, in the final.

The 1939 tournament in Switzerland was the last to be played before the outbreak of World War II. The Trail Smoke-Eaters, coached by Elmer Piper from Saskatoon, left Canada in November on a monumental six-month tour, which eventually would bring them to Switzerland for the world championship.

It was an epic adventure for the team from British Columbia's famous smelter-town. Barnstorming all over Europe, they played a total of 71 games. In their exhibition games, they lost only one and had one draw. However, in the world tournament, they swept all eight games.

The Smokies scored 42 goals in the tournament, giving up only a single goal in eight games. It was a performance that came close to the University of Manitoba Grads' feat of refusing to give up even one goal in their schedule of five games in 1931.

When I visited the newly opened Intercontinental Hotel at Prague in 1974, the *maître d'hôtel* emerged from his office carrying a faded photograph. It was a picture of the Trail Smoke-Eaters of 1939. In Prague, the hockey fans still remembered the Smokies.

After the War, having won the Olympic Games of 1948, Canada must have felt some obligation to go to the first post-war world tournament at Stockholm in 1949. The Ottawa Senators didn't win the championship. They settled for second place, after losing to the Czechs and being tied by Sweden and Switzerland.

Next came three successive winners from Canada: the 1950 Edmonton Mercurys at London; the Lethbridge Maple Leafs at Paris in 1951; and the Edmonton Mercurys at the 1952 Olympics in Stockholm.

The Lethbridge Maple Leafs, 1951 world champions.
Hockey Hall of Fame

For some strange reason, 1953 was not a vintage year for world hockey tournaments. Canada didn't send a team to Switzerland. The United States also neglected to send a team. In the midst of play, the "A" Group was reduced to only three teams when the Czechs, who had lost their third match to Sweden, were called home after the president of their country, Klement Gottwald, died suddenly.

All this was leading up to the first appearance of the Soviets on the international hockey scene in 1954. No one in Canada had been forewarned that a new era was about to dawn.

The Soviets, who had been testing themselves as early as 1948, had planned their long-range campaign very carefully. They never had any intention of tackling the major powers until they had developed a team which, they believed, was almost certain to win. Anatoli Tarasov, their longtime coaching genius, has implied as much in his book, *Russian Hockey Secrets.*

In 1948, the Soviets had invited a Czech club-team from Prague to come to Moscow for a hockey clinic, which included exhibition games. Tarasov and his associate, Arkady Chernyshev, were playing-coaches on the Soviet Army team which engaged in those first matches. Two other members of the pioneering Soviet team were Usevolod Bobrov and Anatoli Seglin. Bobrov is remembered as the greatest European star of his era, and he was coach of Team Soviet in the famous 1972 Summit Series. Seglin became an international referee of dubious distinction and later spent many years as equipment manager for the Soviet National Team.

The Soviets had been finely tuned for their appearance at Stockholm. They had copied the master plan given to them by the touring Czechs in 1948. In the intervening six years, they had developed their own style of hockey. It was, in some respects, reminiscent of the free-wheeling, pattern-passing style of the New York Rangers' Frank Boucher-Bill Cook-"Bunny" Cook line of 25 years earlier.

The CAHA was unjustly maligned for sending the Toronto Lyndhursts, a "relatively unknown team," to the 1954 tournament in Stockholm. The Lyndhursts have been unfairly criticized, too. They weren't a poor hockey club by any means. They bumped into a hornet's nest in Sweden. It was their misfortune to be remembered as "the first Canadian team to be beaten by the Russians."

To give the Lyndhursts their due, it is necessary to re-examine the complete schedule of that tournament in Stockholm. Actually, the results of the first seven games played by the Canadian and Soviet teams in the round-robin series left the impression that the Lyndhursts were as good as the Russians — or, possibly, even a bit superior to the Russians. The Canadians won all seven of their games, coming up to the final. They had scored 57 goals, while giving up only 5 goals. They had hammered the Swedes, 8-0. In contrast, the Soviets had been held to a 1-1 tie by Sweden. In their first seven games, the Russians had scored 30 goals, while giving up 8 goals.

Comparing the results of each team's game against the Swedes, the Lyndhursts should be excused for believing that they weren't any worse than an even-money shot against the Soviets in the final. Calm reappraisal of the circumstances suggest that the Soviets had been holding something in reserve for their meeting with the Canadians. Be that as it may, the Lyndhursts certainly were surprised by the speed and efficiency of the Russian assault. The final score was U.S.S.R. 7, Canada 2.

Typically, Canadian sports fans and the Canadian news media reacted as if they, personally, were the direct victims of a national calamity. As had become customary in such catastrophes, the poor old CAHA bore the brunt of the criticism from press and public. The gist of the complaining was: "How could the CAHA have been stupid enough to send a second-rate team to Stockholm where, obviously, the well-prepared Soviets were lying in ambush?" It was a classic example of hindsight being 20-20 vision. In their hour of enforced mourning, the hockey fans in other parts of Canada took some wry consolation from the fact that the losing team came from Toronto. In the eyes of the monumentally disgruntled, the combination of Hogtown and the CAHA would be enough to screw up a two-car funeral. It is even possible that some elders among the disenchanted remembered Harold Ballard's Toronto Nationals of 1931.

Not since the Olympics of 1936 had there been a hockey defeat that cut so deeply into the Canadian psyche. The hockey fans thirsted for revenge. Just around the corner were the Penticton Vees, who were emotionally prepared to be the agents of that reprisal.

In 1955, Penticton, then a town of 14,000 in the peach-belt of southern British Columbia, won a reputation as the hockey capital of the country. A rollicking group of reinstated professionals and hard-shelled amateurs went from Penticton to West Germany with the sole intention of settling accounts with the Soviets.

The Penticton Vees won the Allan Cup shortly after the Toronto Lyndhursts had been unfrocked in Stockholm. Even while they were in the heat of a bitterly contested Allan Cup series with the Sudbury Wolves, in 1954, the Vees were setting their sights on the 1955 world tournament, which would be played in West Germany. In their eagerness, the Vees regarded the Allan Cup series primarily as the one great obstacle in their campaign to exact vengeance from the Soviets.

The Warwick brothers — Grant, Bill and Dick — were the backbone of the robust Vees. The Warwicks had grown up, financially strapped, in Regina during the Depression. Bill Warwick used to recall grimly, "Our house was on the northern outskirts of the city — the last house on the landscape. When we opened our back door in winter, we were hit by an icy wind that came all the way from the North Pole." Grant Warwick, who had been the NHL's rookie-of-the-year with the New York Rangers in 1942, was the playing-coach of the Penticton Vees, and he established the standards of on-ice deportment, which were rather physical, to say the least.

For the Warwicks and their teammates, the trip to West Germany wasn't merely the greatest hockey assignment of their lives — it was a sacred pilgrimage to restore our national pride.

From the outset, the Vees didn't act like members of the Canadian diplomatic corps. On the ice, they hit anything that moved. Before the tournament had

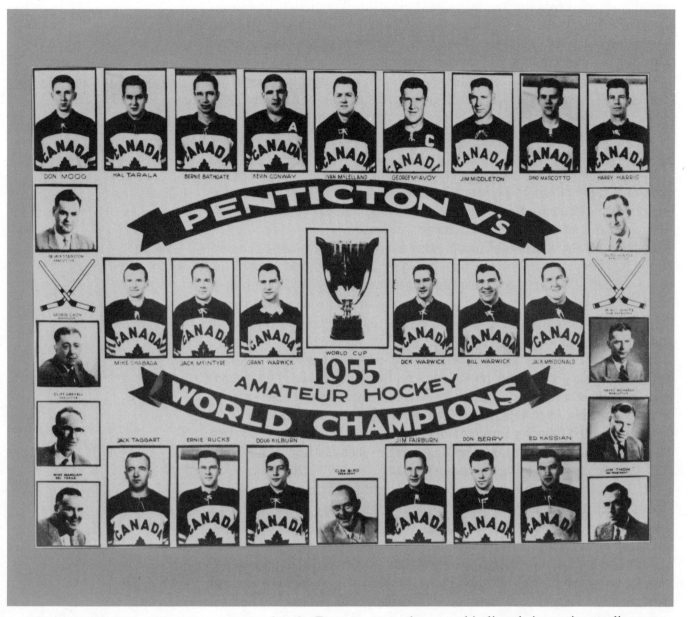

The Penticton team of 1955.
Hockey Hall of Fame

gone very far, the European crowds were whistling their passionate disapproval of these tactics, and Bill Warwick narrowly missed being hit by a liquor bottle (empty) which had been thrown by a fanatic.

The Vees didn't give a damn if the Europeans disliked them. Penticton's forte was slam-bang, hard-skating, hard-hitting hockey, and they had come a long way from British Columbia to demonstrate that the Canadian style still was best.

The entire population of Canada was keyed up for this one. The unfortunate Toronto Lyndhursts hadn't attracted the companionship of any Canadian media reporters when they went to Stockholm. The Penticton Vees' assault on West Germany provoked the presence of a large crowd of media-types, who gave the 1955 world tournament the type of blanket coverage that had never before been devoted to a hockey tournament, anywhere!

Even Foster Hewitt became so excited that he felt impelled to desert his gondola in Maple Leaf Gardens and follow the Battling Warwicks to Europe. In a story which he wrote later for the Toronto *Star Weekly*, Foster said: "I was so determined to attend the hoped-for restoration of Canada's hockey sovereignty that I had arranged to fly to Europe and broadcast the final game, *at my own expense*, through my own CKFH station." Foster was a fine gentleman, but his friends in the news media always chortled over the fact that Hewitt was "very slow" when it came to picking up a luncheon tab. The fact that Foster was prepared to spend his own money gives some idea of the national significance of that final game.

At any rate, Foster was spared the pain of digging into his own pocket for his plane fare. Imperial Oil, Foster's regular sponsors, felt that the world tournament final was of such importance that it should be carried live from Krefeld, West Germany, on the entire CBC radio network.

The response back home in Canada was astounding. The game of Sunday, March 6, 1955, was said to have been heard by the largest audience in the history of Canadian radio, up to that time. The final was played in the evening but, because of the difference in time zones, most Canadians were listening to it on Sunday morning. A Vancouver cleric interrupted his church service to announce the final score.

The Canadian victory wasn't pretty, but it was efficient. Although the Soviets had some truly great hockey players, including Bobrov and Nikolai Sologubov, who were at the peak of their careers, they had never been exposed to the type of close-checking they received from the Penticton Vees.

More than 10,000 hockey nuts crammed the little Krefeld Arena, which had been designed to hold only 8,000. The 2,000 "extras" included Canadian Armed Forces servicemen and servicewomen who were stationed at NATO bases in West Germany. The ear-splitting noise was continuous from the opening face-off until "O Canada" was played on the public-address system during the presentation of the championship trophy.

The game was only four minutes old when Mike Shabaga scored for Canada after he had been set up by Jim Fairburn. In the second period, Canada added two more goals, one by Bill Warwick. In the third period, Canada made it a rout with another two goals, one of which was scored by Bill Warwick. The final score was 5-0.

The Penticton game plan had been designed to contain Bobrov, who personally had destroyed the Lyndhursts the previous year. Penticton's defensive tactics were so effective that Bobrov didn't have a single shot on the Canadian net throughout the entire game.

For the Canadians in the Krefeld crowd, the *pièce de résistance* was a bodycheck delivered by the Canadian captain, George McAvoy, to the Soviet captain, Bobrov. It was the grand-daddy of all bodychecks. Bobrov, knocked high in the air, somersaulted before he landed on the ice, head first.

The swashbuckling Vees were national heroes. Immediately after they had returned to their hotel from the Krefeld Arena, they received telegrams of congratulations from Governor General Vincent Massey, Prime Minister Louis St. Laurent, Health Minister Paul Martin and Defense Minister Ralph Campney.

Left: Harry Sinden as captain of the 1958 Whitby Dunlops. *Hockey Hall of Fame* **Right: The 1958 Whitby Dunlops team.** *Hockey Hall of Fame*

The next day, the House of Commons recognized the feat of the Vees by giving the hockey players, *in absentia*, a standing ovation. The team's trip home from West Germany to Penticton was a triumphal procession, and the little town in the Okanagan Valley has never fully recovered from the most thrilling day in its history.

There is an after-piece to the Krefeld story. After the final game, the Vees were presented with the official trophy of the world championship — a large silver cup — which they bore home in triumph to Penticton. Approximately ten months later, the Warwicks received an overseas telephone call from the IIHF, requesting them to return the cup so that it could be presented to the winners of the forthcoming 1956 tournament. The Warwicks duly sent a silver cup to Europe, but it wasn't the authentic world championship trophy.

The Warwicks had asked a Canadian jeweller to produce a replica of the World Tournament Cup. It was the replica that was sent to Europe. The authentic world trophy remained in Canada. For many years, it was on carefully guarded display in a restaurant which the Warwick brothers operated in Edmonton. Now, the original trophy is in a safety-deposit vault in Edmonton.

"We won that trophy from the Russians," said Bill Warwick. "And we were damned if we were going to give them another chance to hold it."

The national euphoria dissipated quickly the following year when the Kitchener-Waterloo Dutchmen went to the Olympic Games in Cortina, Italy, and finished in third place, behind the Soviets and the Americans. Then Canada decided to ignore the world tournament of 1957 when it was held in Moscow for the first time.

There was still plenty of enthusiastic anticipation in 1958 when the Whitby Dunlops went to Oslo, Norway. The Dunlops were a good solid team, captained by Harry Sinden. It was Sinden's first exposure to the tensions of a world tournament played on foreign ice, and it prepared him emotionally for his task of coaching Team Canada in the 1972 Summit Series.

Once again, the Canadian press corps was out in force for the invasion of Oslo. Foster Hewitt, still tingling from his experience in Krefeld, went along to broadcast the key games to the Canadian public.

As usual, the IIHF officials had seeded the draw to assure that Canada and the Soviet Union would meet in the championship match. The Dunlops responded to the challenge by sweeping their first six games, scoring 78 goals while giving up only 4. The Russians also were unbeaten going into the final day, although they had been tied, 4-4, by Czechoslovakia.

Snow was falling on the open-air arena in the Norwegian capital on the day of the championship, and the condition of the ice deteriorated as the game progressed.

Back home, Canadians listened tensely as Foster Hewitt described the action on radio. The importance of their assignment had over-hyped the Whitby players to such an extent that, while always giving the impression of being the better team, they didn't reach their top stride until the last five minutes of the third period. Finally, Bob Attersley and "Bus" Gagnon broke away to score the goals which assured Canada of a 4-2 victory.

Wren Blair, who was managing the Dunlops, has always insisted that he provided the motivation for that third-period outburst. Attersley was a staunch Conservative, who aspired to a Progressive Conservative nomination in the next federal election. Blair reasoned that, since Attersley was such an ardent rightist, the communist Soviets should be anathema to him.

So, late in the game, Blair walked up behind Attersley, whose performance had been disappointing. He snarled in Attersley's ear, "The way you're playing, I'm beginning to doubt the sincerity of your political convictions." Legend has it (and Sinden confirmed it in later years) that Attersley stormed off the bench for his next shift and promptly scored the go-ahead goal for Canada.

In 1959, Canada was represented by the Belleville McFarlands at the world tournament held in Czechoslovakia. The playing-coach of the McFarlands was Ike Hildebrand and the business manager was Billy Reay. In addition to his hockey prowess, Hildebrand was one of the best lacrosse players in the history of this country and, in 1985, he was voted into the Canadian Sports Hall of Fame. Reay, who had played for Montreal and Detroit in the NHL, later would be coach of the Chicago Black Hawks for 12 years.

Ostensibly, the Belleville team was bankrolled by Harvey McFarland, a contractor in the heavy-construction industry. Afterwards it was revealed, to the embarrassment of some municipal officials, that the City of Belleville, Ontario, had made substantial financial contributions to the hockey enterprise.

McFarland indulged himself by playing the role of the gregarious, open-handed Canadian tycoon as the team toured Europe. Before leaving home, he had gone to the bank to obtain a large supply of Canadian silver dollars. At every stop of the tour, he doled out silver dollars to the youngsters who crowded around the hockey arenas.

The McFarlands won the 1959 tournament with a record of seven wins and one loss. They fulfilled the real purpose of their mission by defeating the Soviets, 3-1. They managed to lose to Czechoslovakia, 3-5, in the championship

Benoit of Canada and Krylov of the Soviet Union battle for command of the puck in a 1959 world championship match. *Canapress*

round, but the loss didn't affect the final standings; in the preliminary round, they had beaten the Czechs, 7-2.

After the Kitchener-Waterloo Dutchmen finished second to the United States in the 1960 Olympic Games at Squaw Valley, there was to be only one more world tournament victory for Canada before they rang down the curtain on our long domination of the international scene.

The Trail Smoke-Eaters, who captured the world title at Geneva in 1961, actually won the trip to Switzerland by default. In the previous season, the B.C. team had lost the Allan Cup final to the Chatham Maroons. However, the Maroons turned down the invitation to make the long tour associated with the world tournament. The Maroons chose, instead, to go to a Christmas week tournament in Moscow.

In those circumstances, the CAHA agreed to permit the Smoke-Eaters to go to the world championships, but only on the condition that the team was strengthened by the addition of players from other clubs. Playing-coach Bobby Kromm added four good recruits: defenceman Darryl Sly and forwards Jackie McLeod, Walter Peacosh and Dave Rusnell.

Most of the Trail players worked for the Consolidated Mining & Smelting Company. As one of them said many years later, "We were able to go to Europe only because the Company kept us on the payroll the entire time we were away." And they were away for a long time — three months. They started out in January and played in Norway, Sweden, Finland, the Soviet Union, East Germany, West Germany, Czechoslovakia and Italy before they reached Switzerland, the site of the world tournament. Before they came home, they had played a total of 51 games.

Kromm took a travel-weary team into Switzerland, but they had played themselves into peak condition. Their coach was a fanatic on the subject of physical fitness. His players remember that he'd frequently stage a two-hour practice in the morning when they were scheduled to play a game that night. When he was coaching the Detroit Red Wings, Kromm often used to say that he had never seen an NHL team which was in the top condition of his 1961 Trail Smoke-Eaters.

The Canadians were tied, 1-1, by the Czechs in their first game of the 1961 tournament. Thereafter, both teams won all their games before the final day. The Czechs had beaten the Soviets, 6-4. By this time, Canadian teams had become accustomed to the IIHF rules whereby, in the event that two teams have identical won-lost-and-tied records, the team with the better scoring differential receives the higher placing. In those circumstances, the Smoke-Eaters went into their final game against the Soviets knowing that they must win by a margin of four goals in order to finish in first place, ahead of the Czechs.

The Smokies defeated the Soviets with forechecking. They sent two men into the Russian zone and, throughout the entire game, they harassed Nikolai Sologubov, who at the age of 35 was still the captain and quarterback of the Russian team.

In the third period, Trail was leading, 4-1, and needed only one more goal to win the championship. Sologubov took the puck behind his own net and went

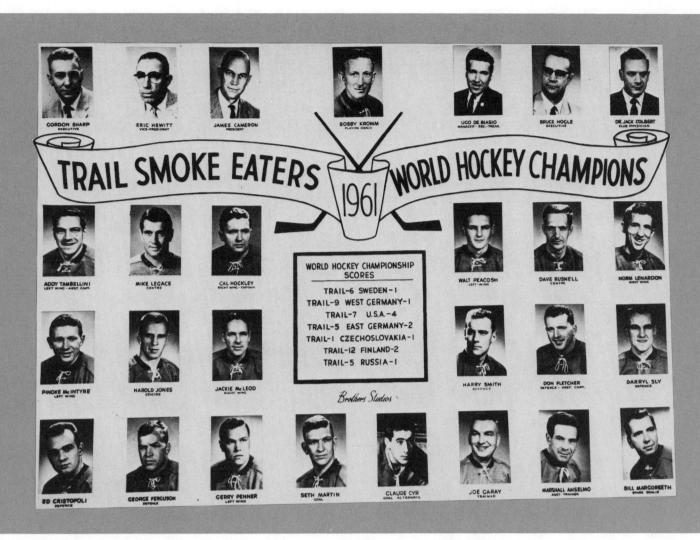

TRAIL SMOKE EATERS 1961 WORLD HOCKEY CHAMPIONS

GORDON SHARP
EXECUTIVE

ERIC HEWITT
VICE-PRESIDENT

JAMES CAMERON
PRESIDENT

BOBBY KROMM
PLAYING COACH

UGO DE BIASIO
MANAGER-SEC.-TREAS.

BRUCE HOGLE
EXECUTIVE

DR. JACK COLBERT
CLUB PHYSICIAN

ADDY TAMBELLINI
LEFT WING - ASST. CAPT.

MIKE LEGACE
CENTRE

CAL HOCKLEY
RIGHT WING - CAPTAIN

WORLD HOCKEY CHAMPIONSHIP
SCORES
TRAIL-6 SWEDEN-1
TRAIL-9 WEST GERMANY-1
TRAIL-7 U.S.A.-4
TRAIL-5 EAST GERMANY-2
TRAIL-1 CZECHOSLOVAKIA-1
TRAIL-12 FINLAND-2
TRAIL-5 RUSSIA-1

Brothers Studios

WALT PEACOSH
LEFT WING

DAVE RUSNELL
CENTRE

NORM LENARDON
RIGHT WING

PINOKE McINTYRE
LEFT WING

HAROLD JONES
CENTRE

JACKIE McLEOD
RIGHT WING

HARRY SMITH
DEFENCE

DON FLETCHER
DEFENCE - ASST. CAPT.

DARRYL SLY
DEFENCE

ED CRISTOFOLI
DEFENCE

GEORGE FERGUSON
DEFENCE

GERRY PENNER
LEFT WING

SETH MARTIN
GOAL

CLAUDE CYR
GOAL ALTERNATE

JOE GARAY
TRAINER

MARSHALL ANSELMO
ASST. TRAINER

BILL MARGOREETH
SPARE GOALIE

This 1961 Trail team was the last Canadian team to win a world hockey tournament in Europe for more than 25 years. *Hockey Hall of Fame*

into a corner, with Dave Rusnell breathing down his neck. The great "Solly" attempted to pass to his young teammate, Alexander Ragulin, but Solly misfired and the puck was intercepted by Norm Lenardon. Lenardon was off-balance. As he was falling, he managed to get away a wrist-shot into a top corner of the net. That shot gave Canada a 5-1 win.

In 1962, the Galt Terriers represented Canada in the world tourney at Colorado Springs, Colorado. Although the Soviets and Czechs were notable absentees, the Terriers finished only second. The Swedes won the championship, beating them, 5-3.

In 1963, the Trail Smoke-Eaters went to Stockholm, but they were only pale shadows of the Smokies who had been so successful in previous invasions of Europe. This time, they finished fourth, behind the Soviets, the Swedes and the Czechs.

Father Bauer's National Team represented Canada in Olympic and world tournament competitions from 1964 through 1969, after which we boycotted world tournaments for eight years.

Canada returned to the world championships at Vienna, Austria, in 1977. The team was made up of NHL "also-rans" collected from clubs which had

been eliminated from the opening rounds of the Stanley Cup playoffs or, indeed, from clubs which had failed to get into the playoffs. Nevertheless, Team Canada '77 had some outstanding personnel, including Phil Esposito, Tony Esposito, Rod Gilbert, young Wilf Paiement and Ron Ellis. The latter came out of retirement to join the squad, which was coached by Johnny Wilson, of the Detroit Red Wings, and Derek Holmes.

The NHL pros, irritated by the European officiating, reacted stupidly in the early games and penalties cost them dearly. However, settling down, they improved steadily in the final weeks and finished a bang-up fourth after administering an 8-3 beating to Czechoslovakia and a 7-0 shutout to Sweden in the championship round.

The NHL players — most particularly, Phil Esposito — were indignant when Gunther Sabetski, president of the IIHF, ordered them to wear helmets in all games. Esposito's outraged screams could have been heard all the way to Sault Ste. Marie, but he wound up wearing a helmet almost as large as a wastepaper-basket.

After they had routed Sweden in their final game, the Canadians stood at attention on the ice while the public-address loudspeakers blared "O Canada." As the last strains of the national anthem echoed in the arena, Esposito hurled his helmet high into the crowd. The helmet was caught deftly by Iona Campagnolo, Canada's minister of health and welfare, who was standing next to President Sabetski.

"Wasn't that nice of Phil?" the minister remarked. "He threw me his helmet as a souvenir."

When the minister's comment was relayed to him, Phil growled, "I wasn't aiming at the lady. I was trying to hit that s-o-b Sabetski, who was standing next to her."

Alan Eagleson and Hockey Canada gathered together another team of NHL also-rans to go to the championships in Prague, Czechoslovakia, in 1978. This squad, coached by Harry Howell, Marshall Johnston and Jean Pronovost,

Above: The 1978 Canadian team won the bronze medals at the world championship in Prague, Czechoslovakia. *James Lipa*   Right: IIHF president Gunther Sabetski and Guy Lafleur. *James Lipa*

played with considerably more discipline than had been displayed by their 1977 predecessors. They won the bronze medals when Pat Hickey, of the New York Rangers, scored the winning goal to defeat Sweden, 3-2, in their final match.

The 1979 tournament in Moscow was a downer for Canada. A mediocre squad, coached by Johnston and André Boudrias, finished fourth.

Following the Olympic Games of 1980, the world tournaments were resumed in Sweden in 1981. To say the least, Canada's team was a colourful crew, coached by loquacious Don Cherry and managed by hard-nosed John Ferguson. However, they failed to win any medals.

Most of the excitement was provided by Barry Long, normally a docile

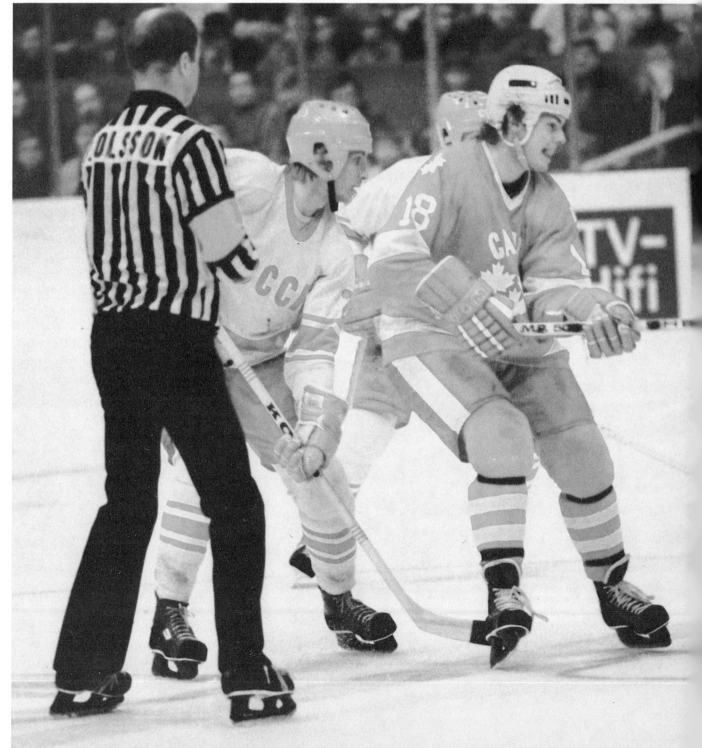

Left: Guy Lafleur, coach Don Cherry and Larry Robinson at the 1981 world tournament. *James Lipa* Below: The 1983 world tournament action. *James Lipa*

Winnipeg Jets defenceman, who gave a boisterous reception to any Eastern Bloc forwards who ventured over the Canadian blueline. In addition, Coach Cherry roguishly needled his European counterparts into a state of wide-eyed exasperation at almost every post-game media conference.

Guy Lafleur made his only world tournament appearance at Stockholm, Sweden, in 1981, and he lasted less than one minute. On his very first shift, Guy was blind-sided and concussed by Rik Van Gogh, a former Ontario Junior-B player who was performing for Holland. Lafleur never saw what hit him; probably his vision was impaired by the ill-fitting helmet which the IIHF rules compelled him to wear for the only time in his professional career.

Upsets in the opening round of the 1982 Stanley Cup playoffs enabled Canada to send a genuinely outstanding squad to Finland. When Edmonton, Philadelphia and Montreal were eliminated, coaches Marshall Johnston, Dave King and Red Berenson acquired the services of such fine players as Wayne Gretzky, Kevin Lowe, Bob Gainey, Bill Barber and Darryl Sittler.

The Canadians certainly were the favourites of the crowds in Helsinki and Tampere, Finland. However, they failed to defeat the slick Soviets in two attempts, and, almost inexplicably, they were tied, 3-3, by Italy. They were forced to settle for the bronze medals. The Czechs finished ahead of them — by only one point — when the Russians contrived to play to a scoreless draw with Czechoslovakia in the last game of the tournament. While the Helsinki crowd booed and whistled derisively, the high-scoring Soviets appeared to be strangely unmotivated as they virtually made a gift of the silver medals to their Iron Curtain neighbours.

The 1983 tournament in West Germany saw Canada represented by a team which was coached by the universities' triumvirate of Dave King, Jean Perron and George Kingston. The Canadians were considerably below the quality of our 1982 representatives, but, again, they won the bronze medals.

Canada finally made a notable improvement in 1985 when the team coached by Doug Carpenter, Tom Watt and Ron Smith finished second and won the silver medals at Prague. In the preliminary round, Canada's bright spot was a 4-4 tie with the Czechs, but The Big Moment still was to come.

In the championship round, backed by some outstanding goaltending by Pat Riggin of the Washington Capitals, Canada scored a stunning 3-1 victory over the Soviets. Mario Lemieux of Pittsburgh got two goals for Canada and Stan Smyl of Vancouver got the other.

The gold medal match against Czechoslovakia was a familiar story for NHL professionals in European arenas. Canada simply took too many penalties — seven compared with only two for the Czechs. The crusher was a power-play goal by Darius Rusnik in the third period, while Kirk Muller of the New Jersey Devils was serving a penalty for cross-checking. Canadians pointed out that the goal was "at least three feet offside," but it still counted. The Czechs won the championship, 5-3, when Jiri Lala added an empty-net goal after Riggin was benched in the final 90 seconds of the game.

That victory over the Soviet National Team in 1985 at Prague was the first time that Canada had beaten the Russians in a world tournament match since the Trail Smoke-Eaters had won, 5-1, in Switzerland, 24 years earlier. But

Canada vs. the U.S.S.R. at the 1985 world championship. *James Lipa*

it must not be forgotten that, in the 1960 Olympic Games, the Kitchener-Waterloo Dutchmen defeated the Soviet Union, 8-5.

The Moscow climate in April seldom has proved to be particularly stimulating for Canadian hockey players whose clubs have failed to get past the first round of the Stanley Cup playoffs. April, 1986, was no exception to the general rule. However, Team Canada '86, coached by cigar-chomping Pat Quinn, performed quite creditably, and they came home with the bronze medals. They assured themselves of medals when Tony Tanti, of the Vancouver Canucks, scored the deciding goal in a 4-3 win over Finland.

The performance of Team Canada '87 at Vienna was, to say the least, quite bewildering. They flirted with mediocrity in the qualifying round, scratching out three wins and one tie from their seven matches. Then, they soared to a magnificent peak with a scoreless draw against the Soviet Union in the opening game of the championship round. At that juncture, they had a chance to win the gold medals, but they lost their final two matches to Czechoslovakia and Sweden. The Swedes, in the course of winning their first world tournament since 1962, gave the Canadians a humiliating 9-0 whipping.

The inherent flaws in the 1987 team were exposed in their fourth game of the preliminary round when they were upset, 5-3, by the supposedly harmless West Germans. It was the first time that the Germans had ever defeated Canada in a world tournament. The star of West Germany's unexpected triumph was goalie Karl Friesen from Winnipeg. Friesen was born in Germany, but he grew up and learned to play hockey in the Manitoba capital.

For oldtime hockey fans, this evoked poignant memories of the first time that Canada lost an Olympic championship — at Garmisch in 1936. It was another Winnipeg-raised goalie, Jimmy Foster, who completely frustrated the Canadians that year when Great Britain defeated them, 2-1.

Team Canada's collapse against the Swedes at Vienna was difficult to understand in the context of their superb performance against the Soviet Union only four days earlier. The coaching staff — Dave King, Guy Charron and Tom Watt — had prepared a brilliant defensive game plan for the Soviet match, and their players executed that plan flawlessly. The Canadians checked the Soviets to a standstill through the first 40 minutes and, when they switched to a more offensive strategy for the third period, they had more and better scoring chances than the Russians. It was a game that Canada could have won.

When the Trail Smoke-Eaters came home in 1961, no one suspected that Canada wouldn't win another world tournament in Europe for more than 25 years. And we're not likely to win another one until the IIHF decides to stage its international shinny festival before the opening of the NHL schedule or after the completion of the Stanley Cup playoffs. And, if you believe that the IIHF will make either of those concessions to the North American countries of Canada and the United States, you're not being realistic.

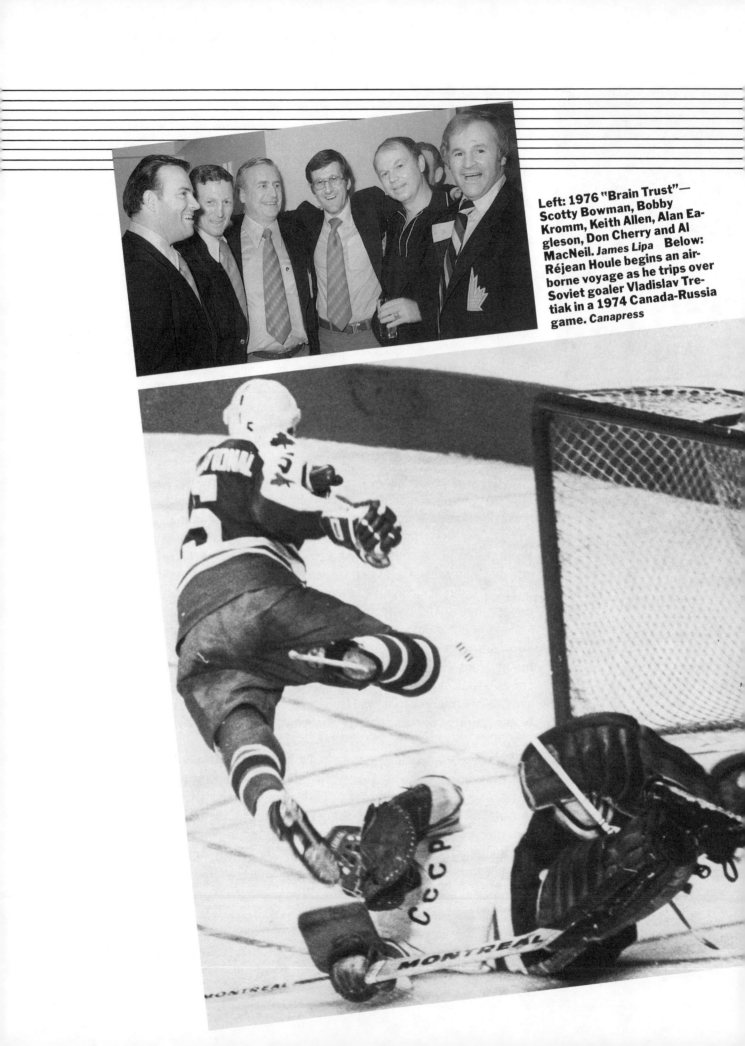

Left: 1976 "Brain Trust"—Scotty Bowman, Bobby Kromm, Keith Allen, Alan Eagleson, Don Cherry and Al MacNeil. *James Lipa* Below: Réjean Houle begins an airborne voyage as he trips over Soviet goaler Vladislav Tretiak in a 1974 Canada-Russia game. *Canapress*

6 THE CANADA CUP

IN THE EYES OF THE GENERAL PUBLIC, THE PRACTICE OF dispatching squads of NHL "also-rans" to Europe for the annual world tournaments may have appeared to verge on imbecility. Although those teams were competitive, they seldom had more than a longshot chance to win the championship. It was the old, old story: "How can you expect to win when 50 percent of North America's best players are still involved in the Stanley Cup playoffs?"

There was, however, a sound financial reason for sending those sacrificial offerings to Europe. In return for our appearance in the world tournaments, the major European hockey powers agreed to come to North America every three or four years to compete for the Canada Cup. It was a simple trade-off, which had been negotiated with the IIHF by Douglas Fisher and Alan Eagleson on behalf of Hockey Canada and the powerful NHL Players' Association. North American currency was the lure which the Soviets, Czechs, Swedes and Finns found irresistible. At the same time, the Canada Cup with its gate-receipts and international television revenues generated handsome profits which were divided equally between the NHL Players' Association and Hockey Canada. The players' share of the profits went into their pension fund. Hockey Canada's share was devoted to nation-wide development programs for the sport.

There were cash prizes for the first Canada Cup, which was played in 1976. Team Canada received $100,000 for finishing in first place in the round-robin tournament and another $50,000 for beating Czechoslovakia in the final. The Czechs received $75,000 for finishing second and another $25,000 as the losing finalists. The third-place Soviets received $65,000; the Swedes were paid $55,000; the U.S. team earned $50,000; and the last-place Finns received $45,000.

The Canada Cup tournament was designed deliberately to capitalize on the tremendous interest that had been generated by the Canada-Soviet Summit Series in 1972. As hosts, the Canadians chose to stage the games in late August and early September, dates which made it possible for them to utilize the services of all their outstanding professionals. Of course, there was the matter of dragging those players off the golf courses and persuading them to attend a training camp.

This time, in the interests of national unity, the NHL made some token concessions to the rival World Hockey Association when Bobby Hull, of the Winnipeg Jets, was named to the 1976 Team Canada lineup. Four years earlier, to the consternation of all hockey fans, Hull had been excluded from the Summit Series because he had jumped from Chicago of the NHL to play in the new league. Bobby Kromm, of the Winnipeg Jets, was appointed one of Head

Coach Scotty Bowman's three assistants. The other two assistants were Don Cherry and Al MacNeil. The most notable addition to Team Canada '76 was Bobby Orr who, while recovering from a knee operation, had missed the entire 1972 series.

The Soviets had become wary after being defeated in 1972. They arrived for the 1976 Canada Cup with a built-in alibi in case they weren't strong enough to win. Deliberately, they hadn't brought five of their best players. Their number one forward-line of Vladimir Petrov, Valeri Kharlamov and Boris Mikhailov was left at home. Two other established stars who didn't make the trip were Alexander Yakushev and Vladimir Shadrin.

Viktor Tikhonov had emerged as the Soviet head coach by this time, although the well-known oldtimer, Arkady Chernyshev, still was associated with him. The two coaches shrugged off questions about the absentees by

Below: 1976 Team Canada goaltender Tony Esposito. *James Lipa* Opposite: Bobby Orr missed the 1972 Summit Series while recovering from a knee operation but played in the 1976 series. *James Lipa*

saying, with straight faces, that they were experimenting with injecting some new, younger players into their lineup.

It was one of those occasions when the Soviets were playing "mind games" with the North Americans. In any event, they arrived with that convenient excuse for possible defeat and, before long, they stole the old Canadian ploy of complaining about the "foreign officiating."

Early in the tournament, the Soviets were tied, 3-3, by the Swedes. The referee was a Canadian, André Lagasse. After the game, the Soviet coaches threatened to withdraw their team and "go home" unless they were assured of

Below: 1976 Canadian team celebrate a win. *James Lipa* **Opposite: Darryl Sittler, 1976 Canada Cup.** *James Lipa*

better officiating in future games. Eagleson, in his capacity as convenor of the tournament, announced crisply that he was prepared to "help the Russians with their packing." They stayed, of course, but in addition to being tied by the Swedes, the Russians were beaten by Canada and Czechoslovakia.

For ardent chauvinists, the high point of the entire show was a Saturday night match between Canada and the Soviets in Maple Leaf Gardens. While the national television audience cracked their knuckles in glee, Canada won, 3-1.

That one victory assured the complete success of the entire enterprise, but it remained for the Czech team and, particularly, their 34-year-old goalie, Vladimir Dzurilla, to capture a large place in the hearts of Canada's hockey fans. Dzurilla had come out of a four-year retirement to play for his national team in 1976. In the round-robin portion of the tournament, the Czechs pulled off a real stunner when they defeated Canada, 1-0, in the Montreal Forum. Fat, old Dzurilla completely frustrated our high-scoring forwards.

Eagleson's tournament plan, which had caused some rumbling among the IIHF brass, called for the first-place team and the second-place team to meet in a two-out-of-three-games playoff. The first game of the finals had been played in Maple Leaf Gardens on Monday, September 13, and Canada had scored a rather easy win, 6-0. The second game, in the Montreal Forum, on Wednesday, September 15, attracted a capacity crowd of 18,040.

The Czech coaches, Karel Gut and Jan Starsi, elected to start the game with Jiri Holicek guarding their nets. When Canada roared away to a 2-0 lead in the opening minutes, the coaches benched Holicek and Dzurilla lumbered off the bench to replace him.

With Dzurilla performing heroics, it proved to be a very exciting game. The Czechs fought back. At the end of the regulation 60 minutes, the score was 5-5. It wasn't until 11:33 of overtime that Darryl Sittler cut in from left wing and scored the winning goal.

After the presentation ceremony, there was an extraordinary scene on the ice. Team Canada players stripped off their jerseys and traded them with the defeated Czechs. Bobby Hull skated up to Dzurilla; he gave the Czech goalie a bear-hug and a big kiss, right on the cheek. All that was rather unusual conduct on the part of North American professionals.

Don Cherry, never a shrinking violet, took credit for the strategy which led to the winning goal. Before the beginning of the overtime, Cherry, who had been scouting the game from the press box, went down to the dressing room and advised Sittler: "After you get over their blueline, fake a shot. Dzurilla will come out of his net. So, shift to your left and go deeper. He will have left you with plenty of open net."

The second Canada Cup tourney was planned for 1980, but it was cancelled at the request of the federal government when the Soviets invaded Afghanistan. This resulted in an American and Canadian boycott of the Summer Olympic Games in Moscow. The tournament was rescheduled for 1981, and although very successful financially, it proved to be an emotional downer for Canadians.

Left: Canada's Marcel Dionne after a goal scored by Bobby Hull in 1976 Canada Cup action in Toronto. *Canapress* **Overleaf: Team Canada's Bobby Clarke pokes the puck between Czech goalie Vladimir Dzurilla's legs in September 15 game of the 1976 Canada Cup.** *Canapress*

Initially, it appeared that Coach Scotty Bowman had assembled the best group of big-shooters ever to represent the NHL. Certainly, the starting forward-line of Wayne Gretzky at centre, Guy Lafleur at right wing and Gilbert Perreault at left wing was the equal of any unit that had yet performed in international hockey. However, things began to go amiss when Perreault, who was emerging as the individual star of the entire shebang, broke a leg while Canada was playing to a 4-4 tie with Sweden in one of the round-robin games. Then, as the tournament progressed, it became apparent that while we had high-scoring forwards, Canada's defencemen lacked the speed and mobility of some of their rivals.

After being tied by Sweden, further evidence that Canada might be in trouble was provided by a 4-4 tie with Czechoslovakia in the Winnipeg Arena. It was a game which, on the run of territorial play, the Czechs could have won.

However, national confidence was restored on September 9, 1981, when Canada defeated the Soviets, 7-3. The enthusiasm proved to be shockingly ill-timed. For that particular game, the Russians had rested Vladislav Tretiak, and he was replaced in the nets by Vladimir Myshkin. On top of that, the final score could have been slightly misleading; the game was a tie, 2-2, into the final period before the Canadians broke loose for five goals.

This proved to be one of those occasions when the best-laid plans go astray. Eagleson, contemplating the horrible possibility that Canada might lose to the Soviets in the round robin, had decreed that four teams should be in the playoffs. In the first round of the playoffs, the first-place team would play the fourth-place team. The second-place and third-place teams also would play off. Then the two survivors would meet in a sudden-death final. Thus, Canada would have had, likely, a second shot at the Russians.

This carefully plotted playoff plan killed us. Canada actually finished the round-robin portion of the tournament in first place. At that point, Eagleson could have said, "We're the champs," and he could have told the Soviets to go home. Unfortunately for us, the niceties had to be preserved. Russia beat Czechoslovakia in one semifinal and Canada, looking far from impressive, beat the Americans in the other semifinal.

All this set up a Canada-Soviet championship game in the Montreal Forum on the afternoon of Sunday, September 13, 1981. Some deflated observers were to refer to this date as "the darkest day in the history of Canadian ice hockey." Certainly, the Soviets had set us up beautifully before moving in for the kill. Tretiak returned to their net that afternoon, and he gave one of his finest performances. The game started out with no suggestion of the complete deflation awaiting Team Canada. There was no scoring until the fifth minute of the second period when Igor Larionov potted the first goal for the Soviets. The confidence of the spectators was restored momentarily when Mike Bossy tied the game at 1-1, but shortly thereafter, Sergei Shepelev scored for the Russians — and the rout was on!

Quickly, it became obvious that the Soviets, aware that the Canadian defencemen were vulnerable, had been "playing possum" when they lost their round-robin game. Now, they swirled around those defencemen as if they were

Above: 1981 Canada Cup action. *James Lipa* Below: Bob Gainey, 1981 Canada Cup. *James Lipa*

stationary fire-hydrants. The Soviets won, 8-1, and they richly deserved their big margin of victory. On that particular afternoon, they were awesome.

The spectators in the Forum deserve credit for staying until the finish. Politely, they remained to applaud while the Soviet national anthem was played and the Canada Cup was presented to Captain Boris Mikhailov. But, frankly, it was galling to accept such a completely demoralizing defeat in a sport which had been invented in this country.

The Russians, after guzzling their customary post-game quota of six Cokes, packed their gear and headed for their bus at the Closse Street door to the Forum. As they were jostling their way out of the arena, someone heard that the Canada Cup Trophy had been packed in one of their equipment-bags and was on its way to Moscow.

Above: Larry Robinson controls the puck in a 1981 Canada Cup game. *James Lipa*
Right: Brian Engblom, 1981 Canada Cup. *James Lipa*

Being apprised of the kidnapping, Alan Eagleson led the charge to retrieve the Canada Cup Trophy. He was aided and abetted by half a dozen members of the Montreal constabulary. After some extremely undiplomatic exchanges, the trophy was retrieved by the irate Eagleson, who shouted that it was "the property of the Canadian Government." Obviously, no one had bothered to tell Eagleson about the occasion on which the Penticton Vees had resorted to subterfuge to keep the original world championship trophy hidden in Canada, after bringing it home from Krefeld in 1955.

The passage of time heals all wounds, and by the time Eagleson got around to planning another Canada Cup series for the autumn of 1984, most Canadians had managed to convince themselves that the horrible events of September 13, 1981, had been merely a figment of their imaginations.

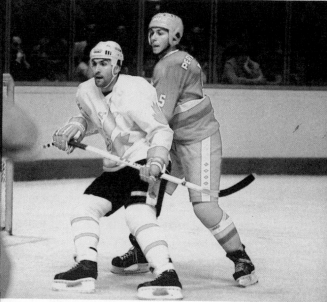

Above: John Tonelli, 1984 Canada Cup. *James Lipa*

Even before the first day of training camp, Team Canada '84 was under fire. Glen Sather, who had been appointed head coach, selected eight of his Edmonton Oilers to play in the tournament. Criticism of Sather's choices wasn't confined to the fans or the sports news media — even Mike Bossy, who ironically was to be a hero of the tournament, felt obliged to fire a few zingers in the direction of the selection committee.

Eagleson, whose tournament playoff format in 1981 would haunt him forever, came up with some amendments for 1984. This time, there would be a sudden-death playoff between the first-place and the fourth-place teams. There'd be another sudden-death game for the second-place and third-place teams. Then there would be a two-out-of-three-games final. This was an attempt to avoid a repetition of 1981 when Canada was clobbered by the Soviets in a single-game final.

It was singularly fortunate that Eagleson again opted for that four-team playoff system, because, to the consternation of the populace, Canada finished fourth in the round-robin phase of the proceedings.

This time, all the games were played in Western Canadian arenas, particularly the Edmonton Northlands Coliseum and the Calgary Olympic Saddledome. The reason for choosing these sites? The Edmonton Oilers had won the Stanley Cup for the first time in May. And with the Edmonton-Calgary rivalry burning brightly, Alberta had become a hotbed of professional hockey enthusiasm in North America.

Canada's record in the round-robin series was spotty. They defeated the West Germans, but then they were tied, 4-4, by the United States. Before they recovered from that ego-deflator, they went to Vancouver and *lost* to Sweden, 2-4. The dull performances were difficult to explain. The team had gone through a lengthy training camp at Montreal, beginning on August 6. Almost a full month later, some of the players were acting like complete strangers on the ice.

The news media's comments merely echoed the views of the ticket-purchasing spectators and the national television audience. The gist of it was: "This is shocking. This is going to be another debacle, like 1981." Sather and his players deflected some of the heat from themselves when, after losing to Sweden, they rebounded to defeat Czechoslovakia, 7-2. However, they took another downturn in their final match of the round robin when the Soviets gave them a 6-3 thrashing.

For Canadian spectators, this was unbelievable! Playing in the arenas of their own country, Team Canada had finished fourth — behind the Soviets, the Swedes, and even the Americans. Fortunately, the playoff format would give the fourth-place Canadians one more shot for all the marbles.

In the first playoff game, which didn't attract a capacity crowd, the Swedes defeated the United States, 9-2. Then on the night of September 13, 1984, the new Calgary Saddledome was sold out completely as the Canadians had the opportunity to redeem their battered reputation in a sudden-death shootout with the Russians.

It proved to be a magnificent exhibition of hockey, played at tremendous pace from start to dramatic finish. The speed of the game, the crispness of the passing and the brilliance of the two goaltenders, Pete Peeters and Vladimir Myshkin, had the "live crowd" in a constant uproar while televiewers were rooted to their chairs. From the outset, there was a strong feeling that a "break" would decide the outcome.

After a scoreless opening period, Team Canada really caught fire in the next 20 minutes. In retrospect, the Canadians should have had their opponents buried before the end of that second period; they outshot the Soviets, 17-6. However, they managed to score only one goal on Myshkin. And, at that, it resulted from a power play while defenceman Zinetula Biljaletdinov was serving a penalty.

The third period began in a fashion which suggested that the Canadians might have shot their bolt. Svetlov scored at 5:19 while Larry Robinson was in the penalty box. Less than two minutes later, the Soviets took a 2-1 lead when Sergei Makarov flitted through the defence like a will-o'-the-wisp to baffle Peeters with a rising shot.

Canada lived to fight again when Doug Wilson, of the Chicago Black Hawks, forced the game into overtime by scoring at 13:59 on assists from Wayne Gretzky and Bob Bourne.

The Soviets had never had any previous experience with overtime, but you wouldn't have guessed as much when you consider the manner in which they played. Actually, they could have won the game in overtime if Paul Coffey hadn't broken up a two-on-one breakaway by making a poke-check interception of a pass.

The end came without warning. John Tonelli, who had been Canada's best worker over the course of the tournament, made what must have been his one thousandth sortie into the left-wing corner in pursuit of the puck. He dug out the puck and got it back to Coffey on the left point. Coffey really didn't have time to get set for a shot and, under pressure, he fired in the direction of the Soviet net. Bango! The puck was in the net and Canada was the 3-2 winner after 12 minutes and 29 seconds of overtime.

The shot had been deflected into the net by Bossy's stick. Bossy said later: "The goal was an accident. I was at the side of the net and the puck hit my stick, halfway up the shaft. I didn't even see the puck coming." For his part, Coffey said: "All I saw was three white shirts (Canadians) in front of the net and I let a wrist-shot go. I don't think that the shot even was going to be on the net." Until the videotapes of the game were studied later, no one appeared to have noticed that two Soviets, goalie Myshkin and defenceman Biljaletdinov, had lost their sticks.

Still, nothing could obscure the fact that, despite the close score, Team Canada had much the better of the territorial play over the night. Throughout the 72 minutes and 29 seconds, the Canadians outshot the Russians, 41-23. I can remember only two other occasions on which an NHL team outshot a Soviet team by such a wide margin. At the Montreal Forum, on New Year's Eve, 1975, the Montreal Canadiens outshot Moscow Red Army, 38-13, as the

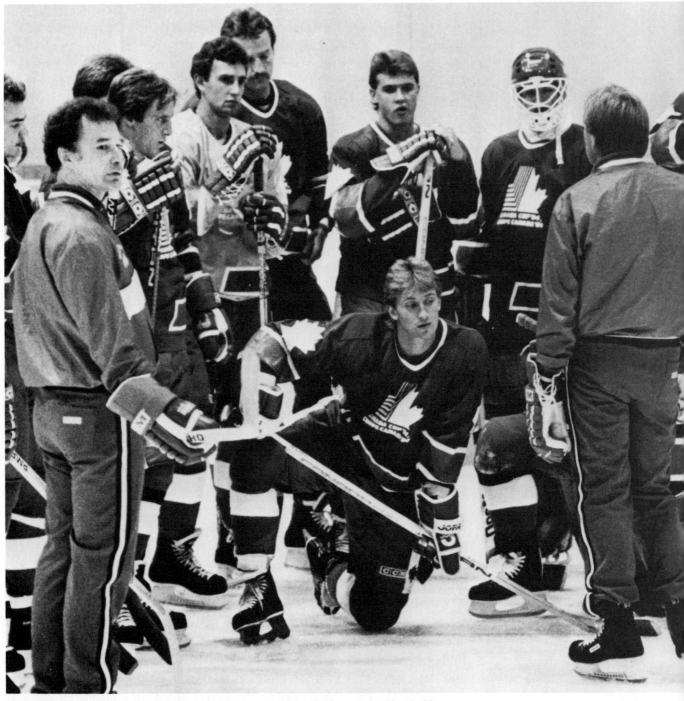

Team Canada coach Glen Sather gives players a blast during a practice in Vancouver following the team's 4-4 tie September 4, 1984, with Team U.S.A.
Canapress

teams played to a 3-3 draw. Eleven nights later in Philadelphia, the Flyers outshot Red Army 49-13 while hammering out a 4-1 win.

After all the intense emotion of Canada's win over Russia in the 1984 Canada Cup semifinal, the final series with Sweden was, not unexpectedly, anticlimactic. The final had been scheduled for three games, but Canada required only the first two games to wrap up the championship. On the Sunday afternoon following their win over the Soviets, the Canadians were much the better team, winning 5-2. Two nights later, in Edmonton's Northlands Coliseum, the Swedes gave an improved performance, but Canada won, 6-5.

Father David Bauer and Alan Eagleson. James Lipa

THE HISTORY OF HOCKEY CANADA

IN THE LATE 1960S, HOCKEY HAD BECOME A SUBJECT OF NATIONAL concern. A decade of public disenchantment with Canada's continuing defeats in international competitions had culminated in the disappointing third-place finish of Father Bauer's National Team at the 1968 Olympic Games in Grenoble, France. The noisiest voices in the sports news media were yammering incessantly about Canada's lost prestige in the hockey arenas of the world. In Ottawa, federal politicians were constantly being reminded by the public that "something must be done about this."

Prime Minister Pierre Elliott Trudeau, whose government was seeking re-election in 1968, responded to the nation-wide clamour. He took official notice of the worsening situation when he delivered a campaign speech at Selkirk College, in Castlegar, B.C., on June 3, 1968. In the course of his speech, the Prime Minister said, "Hockey is considered our national sport and yet, in the world championships, we have not been able, as amateurs, to perform as well as we know we can."

Trudeau's use of the word *amateurs* was deliberate. He, along with most of his countrymen, reluctantly accepted the evidence that Canada's amateur hockey teams no longer could defeat the Soviets or the Czechoslovakians on a regular basis. The time had come for top-class professional players to represent Canada internationally.

In his speech, Trudeau promised, if re-elected, to establish a Task Force on Sports, which would be empowered to investigate all aspects of amateur sports in Canada. The Prime Minister honoured his pledge. After the Liberal Government had been re-elected, they appointed a three-member task force, with instructions to conduct an exhaustive coast-to-coast study.

This was not the first occasion on which the federal government had taken an official interest in sports. Back in 1961, the administration of Prime Minister John Diefenbaker established the National Fitness Council, under the direction of J. Waldo Monteith, the minister of health and welfare.

The National Fitness Council's budget, for financial support of the various amateur sports programs, had been limited to $5 million annually. The Fitness Council never came close to spending its allotted budget until the fiscal year of 1966-67; in gearing up for the 1968 Summer and Winter Olympic Games, it provided $4,665,769 to prepare Canada's athletes for their international competitions.

However, when the task force was appointed in 1968, the members were given an understanding that their recommendations would receive the full financial support of the federal government. This time, the government was prepared to implement a program which would enhance Canada's image in the international sports world as well as provide programs for the improvement of athletic disciplines at the domestic level.

111

The chairman of the task force was Dr. W. Harold Rea, a prominent Torontonian with a record of outstanding accomplishments in the oil industry. Dr. Rea's co-members were Dr. Paul W. DesRuisseaux, of Quebec City, and Nancy Greene, of Rossland, B.C. Dr. DesRuisseaux was a former Canadian champion in several sports and a widely recognized authority in the field of sports medicine. Nancy Greene was, of course, the greatest female skier Canada had ever produced.

Nancy Greene's appointment to the task force was appropriate. Trudeau's campaign promise had been made at Selkirk College where she was a student. On that occasion, he had recognized her, personally, as a two-time world champion and the winner of a gold medal and a bronze medal at the recent Olympic Games in Grenoble, France.

The director of administration for the task force was Christopher H. Lang, a 27-year-old Hamiltonian, who, while working for Citibank in New York, had called Dr. Rea to offer his services. Twenty years later, Lang still is the secretary-treasurer of Hockey Canada. He is the only individual who has been involved continuously with the offshoots of the Task Force Report.

The members of the task force worked speedily, and since they had a clear idea of where they were heading, they worked very efficiently. They travelled from coast to coast, giving every sports group the opportunity to express pertinent views. Additionally, they interviewed prominent representatives of the Canadian business community, soliciting their opinions of the future of hockey and other sports.

The task force was named on August 2, 1968, and less than seven months later — on February 28, 1969 — its extensive report was tabled in the House of Commons by John Munro, the minister of health and welfare. The report, which was an outstanding example of let's-get-to-it practicality, was written — without fee — by two of Canada's most able sports historians: Douglas Fisher, the former MP for Port Arthur, and Professor Stephen F. Wise, of Carleton University.

The task force had received heavy media coverage when it conducted hearings across Canada. Even the prime minister and the minister of health and welfare must have been agreeably surprised by the equally massive media attention that the Task Force Report received when it was unveiled at a press conference on the same day that it was tabled in the House of Commons. The television networks gave it top billing on their national news programs. The newspapers sent not only their sports commentators, but also their national news columnists to cover the event. It received almost as much attention as a budget speech. The media reactions were positive and warmly enthusiastic.

Although the task force recommended the formation of "Sport Canada" to embrace all amateur sports organizations in the country, the main thrust of the report was aimed at hockey. It said, "We recommend that a non-profit corporation, to be known as Hockey Canada, be established for the purpose of managing and financing the National Hockey Teams of Canada."

The report left no doubt that, in the view of the task force members, the Canadian Amateur Hockey Association must be prepared to delegate some of

Left: Christopher Lang, secretary-treasurer of Hockey Canada. *James Lipa* **Above: Douglas Fisher, former chairman of Hockey Canada.** *James Lipa*

its long-cherished rights to Hockey Canada. Two pertinent recommendations were:

"The CAHA be required to nominate the team selected by Hockey Canada as Canada's representatives in international and Olympic competitions under the jurisdiction of the International Ice Hockey Federation."

And:

"The CAHA should initiate steps to have the IIHF declare the world championship a bona fide "open" competition in order that Canada may be represented by a team of Canada's best players."

The implications were clear. Even as early as 1968, it had become obvious that Canadians wouldn't be satisfied until they were given the right to have the professionals of the National Hockey League playing against the national teams of the Soviet Union, Czechoslovakia, Sweden, *et al*. It was obvious, too, that the federal government was anxious to have all the country's various hockey organizations represented as "partners" in Hockey Canada. While the sporting public applauded this objective, it was viewed with grave misgivings by the CAHA and the proprietors of Canada's two NHL franchises — the Montreal Canadiens and the Toronto Maple Leafs.

John Munro didn't wait for the tabling of the Task Force Report before urging Chairman Rea to take preliminary steps to implement some of the report's recommendations. "Go ahead," he told Rea. "The government is going to back you to the hilt." Accordingly, Rea convened a meeting at the Château Laurier Hotel in Ottawa on December 8, 1968. Although the federal government was providing the clout, Rea invited leaders of the Canadian business community, soliciting their input for setting a new course for Canada in hockey. At this stage, representatives of the government were conspicuous by their absence.

The following day, Rea convened another meeting with a considerably increased cast of characters. The business community was represented by such high-profile Canadians as Max Bell, the wealthy newspaper publisher and international sportsman; Ian Sinclair, chairman and president of Canadian Pacific; and Charles W. Hay, retiring chairman of Gulf Canada. Clarence S. Campbell, president of the National Hockey League, attended in an ex officio capacity, and the Montreal Canadiens and Toronto Maple Leafs were also represented. The CAHA was represented by its president, Earl Dawson, and its executive director Gordon Juckes. Father David Bauer was there, along with Chris Lang of the Task Force staff and Douglas Fisher, co-author of the Task Force Report. It is important to mention that, from the very outset, such business leaders as Bell, Sinclair and Hay insisted that they would never be satisfied until Canada was represented internationally by a team of professionals from the National Hockey League.

From those inaugural meetings, Hockey Canada emerged with a two-fold mandate from the federal government:

1. To support, operate, manage and develop a national team or teams for the purpose of representing Canada in international tournaments and competitions;

2. To foster and support the playing of hockey in Canada and, in particular, the development of the skill and competence of Canadian hockey players.

In the wave of enthusiasm occasioned by the tabling of the Task Force Report, John Munro stepped into the picture, personally, by calling a meeting to be held at the Skyline Hotel in Ottawa. This, in all probability, was the most widely publicized meeting in the history of Hockey Canada. The full thrust of the federal government's intervention was evident on this occasion. Everyone who was important in hockey accepted the "invitation" to attend.

The February 24, 1969, meeting requires a bit of scene-setting. It had become obvious that Alan Eagleson, executive director of the National Hockey League Players' Association, held the key to providing Canada with a team of NHL professionals for future competitions. Stafford Smythe, of the Toronto Maple Leafs, and David Molson, of the Montreal Canadiens, were in attendance, chiefly because they didn't wish to incur the wrath of the federal government.

At that time, Les Canadiens and the Maple Leafs didn't enjoy wide popularity in certain sections of the country, particularly in the West. Many Canadians had been outraged when the NHL expanded from six teams to twelve teams in 1967 and the Montreal and Toronto clubs failed to support Vancouver's bid for an expansion franchise. They may have had other good reasons for their action, but, superficially, it appeared to the Canadian public that Montreal and Toronto had been motivated by greedy self-interest. Possibly, they didn't want to share their lucrative television revenues with a third Canadian team. In any event, Vancouver was turned down by the NHL's 1967 expansion committee. As a result, the products of two prime television sponsors — Imperial Oil and Molson Breweries — had suffered a brief boycott in British Columbia.

Stafford Smythe had another reason for wishing he could avoid John Munro's meeting in Ottawa. Smythe had said publicly that he'd never sit down at the same conference table with Father David Bauer of the National Team. Even Clarence Campbell didn't care particularly for Father Bauer, but in the interest of exhibiting unified national support for Hockey Canada, Campbell was prepared to stomach his personal antipathy.

John Munro was an astute politician. He had invited Douglas Fisher and me to attend the meeting at the Skyline Hotel. Fisher not only was there as co-author of the Task Force Report, but also as the author of a syndicated column on politics. Although I was there as a "consultant" to the department of health and welfare, at the time I was also writing a syndicated sports column which appeared in 13 Canadian cities. Munro surmised — quite correctly, as subsequent events demonstrated — that Stafford Smythe scarcely would refuse to sit at the same table with Father Bauer when his actions were likely to be reported in two syndicated columns.

The meeting progressed flawlessly, and Eagleson, Smythe and Molson became the most important partners in Hockey Canada.

I can't speak for Douglas Fisher, but I had no illusions concerning the reasons for my invitation to that and subsequent meetings of Hockey Canada. I was useful at the time. As a veteran reporter who was fully aware of the meaning of "political expediency," it came as no surprise to me when Hockey Canada quietly dumped me three years later, after my hyperactive typewriter became an embarrassment to them.

When Team Canada was being selected, in June, 1972, in preparation for the Summit Series with the Soviets, some of the American club-owners in the NHL — notably Bill Jennings of the New York Rangers — expressed reluctance to have their players involved in the project. Sitting down at my typewriter, I fired off a few missiles in the direction of Jennings and any other U.S. club-owners who were dragging their heels. Warming up to the subject, I wrote that, in effect, the U.S. club-owners could stuff it! We'd put together a team from the three Canadian franchises — Montreal, Toronto and the Vancouver Canucks — and we'd wax the Soviets without any American assistance.

My rococo prose embarrassed the governors of Hockey Canada, particularly Alan Eagleson and Clarence Campbell, who had the unenviable task of buttering up the U.S. club-owners to assure their support of the Team Canada project. No one said anything to me; I didn't even receive a Dear Jim letter. Simply, I didn't receive any more invitations to attend meetings, and my career as a consultant to the department of health and welfare had ended.

Sixteen years later, I remain an ardent supporter of Hockey Canada. I believe that the formation of Hockey Canada was the best thing that ever happened in

Canadian sports. If today they asked me to perform some trivial task for Hockey Canada, I'd jump at the chance as eagerly as I climbed aboard the bandwagon back in the winter of 1968-69.

From Day One, the representatives of the Canadian Amateur Hockey Association were the most reluctant fellow-travellers under the Hockey Canada banner. It was a partnership that wasn't exactly made in heaven. Earl Dawson and Gordon Juckes could see their own powers being eroded, but they were obliged to go along because their operations were dependent on generous infusions of federal government funds. On the other side, Hockey Canada was forced to have the CAHA as a partner because the CAHA was Canada's official voting member of the International Ice Hockey Federation. And, despite what Canadians might think of the charade, the IIHF professed that all its European member countries played "amateur" hockey.

There were several other developments at that memorable February, 1969, meeting in the Skyline Hotel. It had been Harold Rea who had induced Max Bell, Ian Sinclair and Charles Hay to volunteer their support for Hockey Canada, but it was under John Munro's stewardship that they were put to work, immediately. Bell was elected chairman of Hockey Canada; Hay was elected president; and Sinclair was delegated to head a committee which would seek financial support from the business community.

With an ironic twinkle in his eye, Alan Eagleson professed to be satisfied when the newly appointed governors urged him to be chairman of the public relations committee.

Hockey Canada also selected a general manager. The nomination of Leighton "Happy" Emms was endorsed by all the professional interests who were present, including David Molson of the Montreal Canadiens and the conspicuously amenable Stafford Smythe of the Maple Leafs. Emms recently had been general manager of the Boston Bruins, but was perhaps better known for his ownership of successful junior hockey franchises in Niagara Falls and Barrie, Ontario.

His new Hockey Canada employers reacted a bit nervously to Emms when, almost immediately, he suggested that Jackie McLeod, coach of the National Team, should be replaced by Eddie Bush, of Hamilton. Since Bush, a robust, colourful former Big Leaguer was known to be a coach of exceptionally "physical" hockey teams, there was some concern that his appointment to handle the National Team in international competition might lead to the early outbreak of World War III.

When his nomination of Bush evoked little enthusiasm, "Hap" began to take a closer look at his new job. He discovered quickly that his employers expected him to fly frequently between Toronto and Winnipeg, which was the headquarters of the National Team. Furthermore, they expected him to travel to Europe for world competitions, and he would be obliged to accompany the Hockey Canada delegation to frequent IIHF conferences on the other side of the Atlantic.

None of this appeared to fit in with the semi-retirement schedule that "Hap" had envisioned for himself after leaving the Boston Bruins. He had planned to spend at least two months of each summer cruising in his boat on Lake Simcoe.

Not surprisingly, he resigned, only five months after his appointment.

Emms was replaced by A.J. "Buck" Houle, a nominee of Stafford Smythe. Houle had been a longtime operator of minor league hockey franchises for Maple Leaf Gardens, and he had been office manager for Conn Smythe's sand and gravel business. Houle, a quiet and patient man, served Hockey Canada efficiently through the 1972 Summit Series, after which he became general manager of the Ottawa Nationals and the Toronto Toros in the World Hockey Association.

Within three months of being incorporated, Hockey Canada had its official immersion internationally. Father Bauer's National Team went to Stockholm in April, 1969. As well as the usual CAHA delegates, Hockey Canada had a full representation of "Observers."

In the spring of 1969, the Nationals were, generally, a young team, and they did not fare well at Stockholm. They won only four of their ten tournament games, and they finished fourth in the six-team round robin.

In Stockholm, the five other nations represented in the "A" group of the tournament were keenly aware that, this time, the federal government of Canada had assumed control of the country's hockey destiny. After "Bunny" Ahearne's meeting with Alan Eagleson, there was a subtle change in the attitude of Europe's hockey powers. They began to realize that, if they wished to keep Canada as a member of the IIHF, they must be prepared, ultimately, to have Canada represented in tournaments by the professionals from the National Hockey League. Two months later, at an IIHF meeting in Crans, Switzerland, the Europeans made that first major concession — allowing Canada to use nine minor league professionals and reinstated amateurs.

Later, when any reporters were within hearing, Ahearne would make a point of insisting that, at Crans, he had cast the deciding vote in Canada's favour. However, not one of the Canadian delegates who was present on that memorable occasion, has found fit to corroborate Ahearne's version of history.

Before that meeting in Crans, Hockey Canada Chairman Max Bell had undergone the first of several operations for the removal of brain tumors, and the day-to-day operation of Hockey Canada had become, increasingly, the duty

Max Bell, former chairman of Hockey Canada. *Canada Wide*

of President Charles Hay. It was Hay who headed the Canadian delegation to Crans in the early summer of 1969. He was accompanied by Earl Dawson and Gordon Juckes of the CAHA. Also on the trip, representing Hockey Canada, were Father Bauer, Douglas Fisher and Chris Lang.

When the plane landed in Geneva, several small black chauffeur-driven IIHF automobiles were on hand to take the Canadian delegates to a hotel in Crans. The IIHF chauffeurs at the Geneva Airport made it plain that they were expecting only delegates from the Canadian Amateur Hockey Association. Understandably embarrassed, Dawson and Juckes persuaded the chauffeurs to include Hay in the official party for transport to Crans.

The other three Hockey Canada representatives were left at Geneva Airport to fend for themselves. Chris Lang telephoned an old Winnipeg friend, lawyer Gerry Schwartz, who was working in Geneva for international financier Bernard Cornfeld. Within minutes, Schwartz arrived at the airport in the largest, sleekest Cadillac in all of Switzerland.

The Cadillac carried the Hockey Canada group down the highway at a dizzy clip. They soon passed the little IIHF cars, and they were being ushered to their hotel rooms before the IIHF executives welcomed Dawson, Juckes and Hay at the front door of the hotel. Quite inadvertently, Hockey Canada had established the order of precedence for Canada's representatives at future international conferences.

Of course, Canada's rather unexpected victory at the Crans conference table was short-lived. Within a matter of months, the Soviets and their satellites had their abrupt change of heart, which led to the infamous "double-cross" at Geneva on January 4, 1970. This, in turn, caused Canada to withdraw from international hockey.

In fact, the IIHF had voted to deprive Canada of that 1970 world tournament even *before* the Canadians walked into that meeting at Geneva. Charles Hay and his companions had been informed that the meeting would begin at 9 A.M. When they arrived, they learned that the meeting had been in progress since 8 A.M. "Bunny" Ahearne told the Canadians smugly, "In your absence, the meeting already has approved two motions. We've decided that only amateurs can play in the 1970 world tournament. And, we've decided that the 1970 world tournament will be played in Sweden — not in Canada."

Before they left home, the Canadians had received a tip that a double-cross was in the making. Accordingly, John Munro had called an emergency meeting of Hockey Canada in Toronto several days before the group's departure for Europe. The minister directed his remarks to Dawson and Juckes of the CAHA, who feared that they might be left holding the bag, financially, if Canada withdrew from international hockey. Munro told them flatly that they were going to Geneva with the unqualified support of the Government of Canada. If Canada pulled out of international hockey, the federal government would pay off the $160,000 loan which the CAHA had incurred in guaranteeing the accumulated deficits of the National Team from 1965 to 1969. In addition, Munro guaranteed that the federal government would pick up all bills which had been incurred in planning for the 1970 world tournament.

Charles Hay, former president of Hockey Canada.
Hockey Hall of Fame

The federal government honoured John Munro's commitments. It cost the Federal Treasury more than $350,000 to pay off those CAHA obligations.

The chief casualty of the dénouement of January 4, 1970, was the National Team program. With the disbanding of the team, there was a brief lull at the headquarters of Hockey Canada. However, a staff was involved in the second phase of the mandate which had been granted by the federal government. Already underway were programs for the development of coaching and the fostering of hockey skills at the grass-roots level. Studies were being conducted into the technical and sociological aspects of the sport. A long-standing relationship with Canadian intercollegiate hockey was begun through the support provided for a national college tournament program. And there was also increased development of the scholarship program. In 1973, the Canadian Intercollegiate Athletic Union received membership on the Hockey Canada Board, in the person of Robert Pugh, executive secretary of the college group.

The federal government's public stance was a continuing boycott of international hockey, but Charles Hay was one Canadian who clung stubbornly to the belief that, eventually, the Soviets could be persuaded to play against the NHL All-Stars. As a result of overwork and hypertension, Hay suffered a mild stroke, which put him into a Calgary hospital briefly in 1972. In that emergency, Hockey Canada appointed Alan Scott as managing director to keep the organization operating at full-throttle. Although his friends warned him that he was setting a killing pace for himself, Hay was a man of indomitable will, and between January, 1970, and April, 1972, he and Gordon Juckes of the

CAHA made at least eight trips to Europe and Eastern Europe for the sole purpose of breaking down Soviet resistance.

The breakthrough came without any public warning. In April, 1972, Hay and his CAHA associates were attending an IIHF meeting, which was being held at Prague in conjunction with the 1972 world hockey tournament. To the complete surprise of the Canadian public, the Soviets made a deal with the Canadians. The Russians agreed to meet a team of Canadian NHL players in an eight-game series that September.

The announcement from Prague was hailed rapturously by every hockey fanatic in Canada. The popular view here was that the Canadian boycott had been successful. The Soviets, because they wished to resume playing relations with Canada, were willing to disregard any previous strictures which had been imposed upon the Canadians by the IIHF. Nobody in Canada really gave a damn about any philosophical nuances which might have influenced the Soviet decision. Canadians were interested only in the fact that the Summit Series finally would become a reality in September.

There is some truth to the legend that Charlie Hay had a secret weapon at his disposal when he went to that meeting in Prague. Hay was accompanied by Joseph Kryczka, a prominent Calgary lawyer, who had become president of the Canadian Amateur Hockey Association. Kryczka had been born in the mining town of Coleman, Alberta, of Polish stock, and he had grown up with a working knowledge of all the Slavic languages, including Russian.

Initially, the Soviets were unaware of Kryzcka's background, and no one knows how long it took them to penetrate his deception. In any event, at each day's negotiating sessions, Kryzcka sat in silence while interpreters provided Hay with translations of the Russians' arguments. Meanwhile, Kryzcka was listening carefully to all the Soviet interplay, and after each session, he gave Hay a full report on the private conversations which had passed between them.

Hay always felt that Kryzcka's ability to break the Soviet "code" gave him an important edge in negotiations. It was Hay who later gave birth to the legend that Kryzcka was his secret weapon.

Kryzcka, who became a judge of the Trial Division of the Alberta Supreme Court, enjoys relating an incident which occurred on the final morning of negotiations at Prague. As Kryzcka walked into the room, Andrei Starevoitov, the chief Soviet delegate, pulled out a full bottle of vodka and put it on the table. Starevoitov pointed to the bottle, pointed to Kryzcka and barked one word in English, "Drink."

Joe protested, in English, "I'm a Canadian. We don't drink vodka this early in the morning."

With a glint in his eye, Starevoitov countered through his interpreter, "You're not Canadian; you're Polish. Now, drink!"

Looking back on it now, Kryczka is convinced that the several days of careful negotiating by the Russians in Prague were just so much eyewash. He says, "In retrospect, I'm convinced that even before we arrived in Prague, the Soviets had decided privately that their hockey team was good enough to beat the NHL. They strung out those meetings to get every possible concession concerning the rules under which the games would be played."

The events of September would prove that the Soviets had obtained some rather important concessions, particularly in the area of on-ice officiating. However, before jumping to the conclusion that Hay and his colleagues "traded away too much," it should be remembered that Canada was the instigator of the Summit Series. There was a widespread opinion in our country that the NHL professionals would beat the Russians quite handily. Thus, to persuade the Soviets to play, Canada was willing to make concessions.

For the four games to be played in Canada, the Soviets demanded North American amateur hockey referees, who were licensed by the IIHF. Very specifically, they didn't want to have the games handled by referees from the National Hockey League. And, for the four games in Moscow, the Soviets demanded European referees, who were licensed by the IIHF. Also, for the Moscow games, they demanded the European system of officiating — two referees and no linesmen. No one will ever forget the European referees in the four games at Moscow; they had the members of Team Canada foaming at the mouth in utter exasperation.

All the quibbling and second-guessing over the Moscow officiating by the news media and Harry Sinden and his Team Canada associates was to come later. In the meantime, there was feverish activity in preparation for the Summit Series, which was scheduled to open in the Montreal Forum on September 2. A hockey promotion of this magnitude never before had been undertaken by Canadians. There were so many things to be done, and all the planning had to be accomplished in the hurricane-eye of nationwide publicity.

The public immediately became incensed over the exclusion from Team Canada of Bobby Hull and the other players who had defected from the NHL to the newly organized World Hockey Association. Even the television contract for the eight-game series received critical scrutiny in the media when it was arranged, successfully, by a consortium composed of Alan Eagleson, Harold Ballard and Eagleson's prime client and sometime business partner, Bobby Orr. Actually, the television package produced handsome profits for Hockey Canada and the NHL Players' Association. Such a productive contract probably couldn't have been negotiated by any group that didn't have the combined hockey-business connections of Eagleson, Ballard and Orr.

Hockey Canada was also in charge of supervising the logistics of providing transatlantic flights, hotel accommodation and meals for 2,700 Canadians who wanted to follow their hockey team to the Soviet Union. It proved to be one of the most raucous airlifts in the history of intercontinental transportation. The Soviets pride themselves on their phlegmatic acceptance of tourists, but for eight days in late September, 1972, their facade of indifference was — if not broken — at least dented slightly.

The important thing is that everyone profited from the 1972 Summit Series — the Canadians, the Soviets and the hockey fans throughout the world who had the good fortune to watch some truly magnificent sport on television.

Hockey Canada's share of the profits was $405,000; the NHL received $405,000 and the Canadian Amateur Hockey Association received $100,000. The NHL donated its share to improve the pension fund of the NHL Players' Association.

The 1972 Summit Series was a never-to-be-forgotten first. Not all Canadians remember, in great detail, that Hockey Canada promoted a second Summit Series in 1974.

In the two years since it had first been organized, the World Hockey Association had been clamoring for the opportunity to meet the Soviets in a major hockey confrontation. Hockey Canada, as the agent of the federal government, was obliged to act on the WHA's request for an international competition. After all, five Canadian cities were operating franchises in the WHA.

Team Canada '74 didn't hit a financial bonanza, but it was a highly entertaining project and deserves some space in this informal history of Canada's role in international hockey.

The World Hockey Association had been operating for only two full seasons and, therefore, in the summer of 1974, they didn't have an executive branch with the experience or the well-developed business contacts to set up a genuinely lucrative television contract for their eight games with the Soviets. At the last minute, they swallowed their pride and sought the assistance of Alan Eagleson; however, he came into the picture too late to strike a really profitable deal for them. As a result, Hockey Canada emerged from the 1974 Summit Series with a profit of only $18,000, but everyone who was involved had a good time.

Team Canada '74 featured some of our most picturesque Golden Oldies. Gordie Howe was 46 when he had this first opportunity to perform in Moscow.

Alexander Maltsev attempts a shot at Team Canada goal manned by Gerry Cheevers during opening game between Canada and U.S.S.R. September 17, 1974. *Canapress*

Bobby Hull, who had been excluded from the 1972 series, was 35. Ralph Backstrom was 37, Frank Mahovlich was 36, Pat Stapleton was 34 and J.C. Tremblay was 35. Mahovlich and Stapleton were the only holdovers who had played for the NHL team in 1972.

Until that time, the Soviets seldom permitted a player to perform for their own national team after he had passed the age of 30. Apparently, the Russians theorized that the ability of players declined sharply as soon as they entered their fourth decade. However, the Soviets changed their minds when they watched Team Canada '74 in action. Subsequently, they kept such stars as Boris Mikhailov and Vladimir Petrov in their national lineup until they were 35 or 36.

In the opening game at Quebec City on September 17, the greybeards of the WHA performed in exceptionally sprightly fashion, earning a 3-3 tie. Two nights later, in Toronto's Maple Leaf Gardens, Team Canada skated to a 4-1 victory.

At that juncture, the father-in-law of goalie Gerry Cheevers died, and Cheevers stayed in the East for the funeral. Coach Billy Harris called on "Smokey" McLeod to replace Cheevers for Game Three in the Winnipeg Arena. "Smokey" did not have an outstanding game and the Russians won, 8-5, to square the series.

Rick Smith (No. 17) moves in on the puck with Don McLeod far out of the goal. Soviet players Valeri Kharlamov (No. 17, light sweater) and Alexander Maltsev (No. 10) and Team Canada players Paul Shmyr (No. 18) and Bobby Hull (No. 16) were also in on the play in this 1974 Team Canada-Russia game.
Canapress

In Game Four at the Vancouver Pacific Coliseum, goalie Vladislav Tretiak finally learned why Bobby Hull was still regarded as the most-feared sharp-shooter in professional hockey. After the Soviets had taken a 2-1 lead at 12:45 of the opening period, Hull began to find the range. In the ensuing four and one-half minutes, Bobby fired three goals. Tretiak was pawing the air as the shots zipped past him and went into the net. To Tretiak, the pucks must have resembled small black aspirin tablets. Between Hull's second and third goals, Frank Mahovlich also scored, and the Canadians ended the first period with a 5-2 lead.

That should have been enough to win any game, but the great Soviet team just kept chipping away at that lead. Recovering from the initial barrage, Tretiak became unbeatable in their net. The Soviets picked up a goal in the second period, and, with only four minutes left in the game, Canada still was nursing a 5-3 lead. Then, in less than one minute, Alexander Maltsev and Alexander Gusev scored and the Russians earned a 5-5 tie.

The remarkable thing was that, after the four games in Canadian arenas, the record of Team Canada '74 was slightly better than the record of Team Canada '72. Team Canada '74 was going to Moscow with a deadlocked series — one win, one loss and two ties. In 1972, Team Canada had gone to Moscow trailing in their series with only one win, one tie and two losses. Yet, although the senior citizens from the WHA had been performing heroically, their bubble was about to burst when they invaded the Soviet Union.

In 1972, Team Canada players had been permitted to have their wives fly to Moscow to join them for the final four games. In 1974, the WHA players had a better deal, depending on your personal views of wives accompanying players on hockey trips. In this instance, the WHA players took their wives across Canada, and then the women travelled with their husbands on the direct flight from Vancouver to Helsinki, Finland. The team was scheduled to play exhibition games in Helsinki and Göteborg, Sweden. Remembering the sorry experience of Team Canada '72 in Stockholm, the Hockey Canada strategists deliberately avoided that city in 1974.

The flight from Vancouver to Helsinki had its hilarious moments. The players, their wives, several WHA club-owners and scores of reporters and photographers were jammed into the same plane. Mike Walton, of the Vancouver Blazers, had brought along his father, Bob "Shakey" Walton. His dad was an effervescent former senior amateur of exceptional ability, from Montreal, and he is probably the only man ever to travel from Vancouver to Helsinki without sitting down. For ten hours, he walked up and down the aisle of the plane, gossiping with anyone who would listen to him.

One Canadian player had separated from his wife a couple of weeks before the series began. So, he invited a newly acquired girlfriend to accompany him on the trip to Finland and Moscow. Two or three nights before the series moved to Vancouver, the player and his new girlfriend had a spat. Remembering that a hockey player's best friend is his mother, this particular player took his mother to the Soviet Union.

When we arrived in Helsinki, after what had been an exhausting flight, the players and their wives were sitting on bar-stools in the Hesperia Hotel, waiting to be assigned to their rooms. The wife of one star rested her head on the bar and promptly fell asleep. A reporter brought the wife's slumbers to the attention of her husband. "Don't wake her," warned the hockey player. "This is the first time that she's stopped talking since we left Vancouver."

The veterans from the WHA gave it a really good shot in Moscow. In the final analysis, the younger and better-conditioned Soviets had "the legs" to capitalize on the vast ice-surface of Luzhniki, which, of course, was much larger than the skating area of any North American hockey arena.

The Soviets won Game Five, 3-2, and they came right back to win Game Six, 5-2, when the Canadians lost their cool after running into half a dozen penalties, some of them questionable, in the second period. It is worthy of comment that the referee in Game Six was Viktor Dombrovski, the same gentleman who, as goal-judge, had failed to flash the red light when Yvan Cournoyer scored the tying goal in Game Eight of the 1972 Summit Series.

Tempers got out of control completely as the horn sounded to end Game Six. "Whitey" Stapleton speared a Russian, who had been heckling him. Alexander Gusev threw a hockey stick, butt-first, at a Canadian. Stapleton threw a punch at Referee Dombrovski, who had been responsible for letting things get out of hand.

Valeri Kharlamov, suddenly exhibiting unsuspected linguistic ability, made a particularly slurring remark, in English, to Ricky Ley, a Canadian defenceman. Ley, resenting the remark as defamation of his mother, promptly punched Kharlamov's face into a bloody mass. The Soviets dragged the bleeding Kharlamov to their dressing room, and only six of the Russian players remained on the ice for the customary post-game handshakes.

Before the face-off for Game Seven, the Luzhniki public-address announcer, who happened to have grown up in Manitoba and Hamilton, Ontario, solemnly read a carefully prepared warning. He read it in both languages, but obviously it was aimed at the Canadian visitors. He said, in effect, that any player or spectator who acted indecorously during the game would be arrested and jailed. None of the Canadians appeared to be intimidated by the warning; however, Game Seven did have a bizarre finish. The Canadians should have won, but they were forced to settle for a 4-4 tie.

At 19:59 of the final period, Bobby Hull fired the puck into the net for what should have been Canada's winning goal. The red light (signalling "goal") went on and, almost simultaneously, the blue light flashed, indicating that the period had ended. To the indignation of the Canadian players and fans, the referee and the Soviet timekeeper both ruled that the period had ended before Hull's shot entered the net.

Even the Canadian ambassador to Moscow, Robert Ford, became involved. Ford, who had been standing at ice-level at the opposite end of the arena, told the Canadian news media that he had seen the red light flashing before the blue light began to flash.

The immediate aftermath was hilarity verging on burlesque. Bill Hunter, the general manager of Team Canada summoned the North American news media to an impromptu press-conference in the bowels of Luzhniki. He bellowed confidently that he expected all the Canadian visitors in Moscow to attend a protest rally, which he would organize to be held in Red Square at 9 A.M. the following morning. Hunter was so angry that the incongruity of 2,000 Canadian hockey fans attempting to attract public attention by staging a protest rally within the walls of the Kremlin escaped him completely.

The next day was Sunday. The final game of the series was scheduled for later that afternoon. When Sunday morning dawned bleakly, most of the Canadians stayed in their beds, nursing hangovers. If Bill Hunter went to Red Square, he must have been discouraged by the turnout for his protest rally.

There wasn't anything at stake in Game Eight, because the Soviets had already won the series. Team Canada played very well that Sunday evening, but the Russians prevailed, 3-2.

Although Gordie Howe was 46 when he made that trip, the Soviet spectators were waiting eagerly to see him. They knew all about him, and he didn't disappoint them. Whenever Gordie's large elbows happened to make contact with an opponent, the Soviet fans muttered among themselves appreciatively. As far as the Russians were concerned, Bobby Hull shared top billing with Howe. Whenever they ventured out in public, the two were pursued by young and old Soviets who clamored, politely, for their autographs.

The Soviet hockey strategists were amazed by the nimbleness of 46-year-old Howe and 35-year-old Hull. However, another player who caused them to revise their theories about players who were over 30 was 37-year-old Ralph Backstrom. In all probability, he was the best Canadian over the full series of eight games. After 17 years in major league professional hockey, Backstrom demonstrated that he still could match strides with the swiftest of the young Soviets.

With international competition restored in the 1972 and 1974 Summit Series with the Soviets, Hockey Canada turned to a resumption of playing relations with other European nations. Those negotiations resulted in the first Canada Cup tournament of 1976 when the national teams of the Soviet Union, Czechoslovakia, Sweden, Finland and the United States came to Canada.

These Canada Cup tournaments have proved to be very successful, as entertainment and as a source of revenue. In 1976, Hockey Canada had a profit of $600,000, while another $600,000 went into the pension fund of the NHL Players' Association. The Canada Cup tournaments of 1981 and 1984 also produced excellent financial results. Even the CAHA profited. The CAHA received $1 million plus $300,000 in bank interest, which had accumulated while Hockey Canada and the CAHA had been undergoing a lengthy period of mutual disenchantment.

There was, however, a stiff price in national prestige to pay in return for luring those foreign teams to this country for the Canada Cup. Alan Eagleson struck a deal with the International Ice Hockey Federation. Beginning in 1977, Canada agreed to send a team to compete in the annual world tournaments in Europe.

For Canada, it was an annual "Mission Impossible," because the world tournament is always played in early April. The Stanley Cup playoffs seldom have reached the second round by that date, so Canada is condemned to send a squad of players from teams that were eliminated from the first round of the Stanley Cup matches or, indeed, players from teams that finished no higher than seventeenth in the final standing of the NHL's regular schedule. In some respects, Canadians are forced to play with one hand tied behind their backs. The only redeeming aspect of this arrangement comes in the fact that the Europeans are then committed to send their best to compete in the Canada Cup.

Although Canada's professionals had resumed international competition with the Soviets in 1972, our country continued to boycott Olympic hockey until 1980. Canada did not send teams to the 1972 Olympics in Sapporo, Japan, or the 1976 Olympics in Innsbruck, Austria.

There were several occurrences in 1979 that changed the picture. The Canadian Amateur Hockey Association never had been happy with its subordinate role, and it withdrew abruptly from the board of Hockey Canada. This left Hockey Canada with the responsibility of providing Canada's entry for the Olympic hockey tournaments of 1980, 1984 and 1988.

In 1979, Calgary did not have a professional hockey team. Douglas H. Mitchell, Q.C., the lawyer who later became commissioner of the Canadian Football League, headed a group of Calgarians who proposed to Hockey Canada that Father Bauer's old National Team program should be revived with headquarters at the Calgary Corral. On July 31, 1979, 60 amateur players from all parts of the country assembled at the Corral as candidates for Canada's 1980 Olympic Team.

Charles Hay, the first president of Hockey Canada had always wanted his former hometown to become a national hockey centre. Today, he would be happy to see that his dream has become a reality and that his own son, Bill Hay, is the chairman and national spokesman for Hockey Canada's potent 25-man Calgary Committee.

The Calgary operation becomes more impressive with each passing year. Because the Calgary Flames went all the way to the Stanley Cup finals in May, 1986, the Saddledome Foundation profited by an infusion of $1,200,000. Now, in addition to being the headquarters of general manager and coach David King and his National Team, the Saddledome houses Canadian hockey's Centre of Excellence and the Sports Medicine Centre.

The Centre of Excellence includes the Charles Hay Memorial Library. This is a valuable and growing collection of video films, which, with the co-operation of the CAHA, are available to all hockey clubs, from coast to coast. The films include international matches in which Canada has participated and instructional films for coaches, referees and young hockey players.

Calgary has become the focal point of Canada's research and development programs for our national sport. And, with Bill Hay embracing the spirit of dedication to hockey which was exemplified by his father, this may be the appropriate point at which to list the cast of characters who have played roles in Hockey Canada since its inception in December, 1968.

The organization always has received the emotional as well as the financial support of the federal government. It has reported to a succession of cabinet ministers, including: John Munro, Marc Lalonde, Iona Campagnolo, Steven Paproski, Gerald Regan and, most recently, Otto Jelinek, minister of fitness and amateur sports.

In the same period, the chief executive officers of Hockey Canada have been: the late G. Maxwell Bell, the late Charles W. Hay, Douglas Fisher, Torrance Wylie, Louis Lefaive, Mr. Justice W.Z. Estey and, most recently, Ian H. Macdonald.

John Munro probably is the minister who is remembered best by the public, because it was during his term of office that the Task Force made its report, that Sports Canada and Hockey Canada were formed, and that the federal government gave official recognition to the fact that sports were an important part of our cultural heritage. It was while Munro's party was in power that sports took The Great Leap Forward in Canada.

Munro plunged into the job enthusiastically. His stewardship of Hockey Canada kept him in the public eye for the next four years. He enjoyed the challenge of persuading the National Hockey League clubs, the CAHA and the NHL Players' Association to become partners in the new umbrella organization. He enjoyed being front and centre at the numerous high-profile public meetings, and he was conspicuously successful in inducing powerful and well-known members of the business community to devote their energies to restoring Canada's prestige in the international sporting scene.

It is reasonable to say that, next to Trudeau, Munro became the best-known member of the Cabinet as a result of the national preoccupation with Canada's hockey problems. Before he was shunted off to the Ministry of Labour, Munro had made a lasting impression on the future of sports in this country.

Most of the leading performers who made important contributions to the rejuvenation of our hockey prestige, internationally, were appointed to the Hockey Canada Board during the first couple of years of the Munro regime. Those original appointees included G. Maxwell Bell, Charles W. Hay, Father Bauer, Alan Eagleson, Douglas Fisher, Louis Lefaive and Christopher Lang.

Max Bell was the ideal combination of businessman-sportsman to be persuaded to assume the leadership of this new enterprise. It is just possible that because of his long exposure in the international sporting spotlight, Bell was, as far as the general public was concerned, the most widely known businessman in Canada. Like E.P. Taylor, Bell had become a sports-page celebrity through his involvement in thoroughbred horse racing. However, he had been actively involved in sports long before he bought his first race horse. He had been an all-round athlete at St. John's College in Winnipeg, and he played football and hockey at McGill University. When McGill won the Eastern Canadian intercollegiate hockey championship in 1931, Max was the third member of the team's all-western defence, which included his longtime friends, George McTeer of Calgary and Bert McGillivray of Regina.

Max Bell acquired great wealth through his interests in the energy industry. He also amassed great power as co-publisher of eight of Canada's leading daily newspapers. Yet, he never lost the common touch; the friends of his youth remained the friends of his later years, and the door of his Calgary office was always open to characters from the racetrack, who dropped in to chat.

Bell never drank or smoked, and he was addicted to physical fitness. To the amusement of his friends, when they were imbibing in a hotel suite, Bell was likely to practice his own conception of debauchery by calling room-service and ordering a huge dish of ice cream with scoops of three different flavours. It was sadly ironic that Bell, who always kept his body at the very peak of physical condition, should have succumbed, at the age of only 60, to malignant brain tumors.

With his lifelong interest in all sports, Max Bell was a fairly obvious person to be approached for financial support when Father Bauer began to organize his National Hockey Team. Bell and his business-friend, James Richardson of Winnipeg, were the first major western backers of the National Team project. They also were responsible for raising the money to build the Dutton Memorial Arena as a permanent facility for the National Team at St. John's-Ravenscourt School in Winnipeg. And, although the fact never was publicized, the year that Carl Brewer spent with the National Team after quitting the Toronto Maple Leafs, was financed personally by Max Bell.

It was Bell who persuaded his friends, Ian Sinclair, the chief executive officer of Canadian Pacific, and Charles Hay, the retiring chairman of Gulf Canada, to become involved in Hockey Canada. Charlie Hay had impeccable credentials for that important public role. He had a very sound personal background in hockey, and his interest in the sport had been maintained by his son's professional career as a member of the Chicago Black Hawks.

Hay graduated in civil engineering from the University of Saskatchewan and, back in 1923, he had been the goaltender on the most successful hockey team ever to represent that western university. Although they were a college team, the University of Saskatchewan Huskies won the Western Canada championship in 1923, and they met the Toronto Granites in the Allan Cup final. Some hockey historians have classified the Toronto Granites as the best club ever to represent Canada in the Olympic Games. Nevertheless, with Hay performing heroics in the Saskatchewan net, the Huskies gave the Granites a solid testing before losing the national amateur championship.

Upon graduating from college, Hay worked for Canadian Pacific as a civil engineer before branching into the infant Western Canada oil industry. He built the Highway Refinery at Saskatoon. In due course, his refinery was bought out by Royalite, and Hay went to Calgary with the new parent company. Within a matter of years, Royalite was absorbed by the British-American Oil Company and, later, British-American became Gulf Canada. When British-American was taken over, Hay signed a five-year contract to be chief executive officer of Gulf Canada. It was on the expiration of that contract that Max Bell persuaded Hay to join the businessmen-volunteers who were dedicating themselves to the success of Hockey Canada.

As early as 1971, Charles Hay was stressing to his fellow-governors that the development of new techniques and skills at the grass-roots level was the key to the restoration of Canada's hockey prestige. Even then, he was telling his colleagues that Calgary, with its burgeoning oil economy, would be the ideal location for a facility that would provide the research laboratories for such national programs.

Worn out physically by his relentless campaign to bring the Soviet Union into competition with North America's best professionals, Hay did not live long to enjoy the fruits of those prolonged negotiations. He died shortly after the 1974 Series between the Soviets and the All-Star team from the World Hockey Association.

Charles Hay was succeeded by Douglas Fisher, who remained as chairman of Hockey Canada until 1977. Fisher has long been one of the most compelling figures in Canadian public life. He was catapulted into national prominence in June, 1957. As the C.C.F. candidate for the riding of Port Arthur in the federal election, he scored a stunning victory over the Rt. Hon. C.D. Howe, the bellwether of the Liberal Government. Fisher, who was re-elected in 1958, 1962 and 1963, was an exceptionally able Member of Parliament, whose frequent speeches in the House of Commons seldom failed to attract press gallery attention. He was a persistent goad to whatever party was in power and, indeed, he occasionally skewered his own party, of which he became deputy-leader before he decided to retire from active politics in 1965.

By the time he left the House of Commons, this large, energetic man had achieved added national recognition as a political columnist and television commentator. Fisher had started writing a column for the *Toronto Telegram* in 1963. After the *Telegram* ceased publication, his columns appeared in the *Toronto Sun* and were syndicated to more than 25 other newspapers. A sports-follower since childhood, Fisher developed an increasing preoccupation with athletics, particularly the history of Canada's sporting heritage, as he grew older. In addition to his involvement in newspapering, television commentating and various consulting assignments, he found time to collaborate with Stephen Wise on the massive volume, *Canada's Sporting Heroes*, which is, unquestionably, the definitive compilation of sports history in this country.

As co-authors of the Task Force Report, Fisher and Wise felt that sports had been an unjustly ignored aspect of Canadian culture. In the preamble to the Task Force Report, they wrote, "Sport is one of the few dimensions of Canadian life in which truly national folk heroes have been created and constantly are being created."

Fisher probably was the intellectual conscience of Hockey Canada, although he would brush off such an easy categorization. Because he is a large man, physically, and because he takes a puckish delight in projecting an aura of irascibility, some people have found him to be intimidating. The truth is that he has a sparkling sense of humour, and he is, himself, one of those sporting "characters" about whom he has written with affection. Among other things, his Hockey Canada colleagues have found him to be an unusual and entertaining travelling companion.

While other men are inclined to pack an elaborate wardrobe for a two-week trip to a world hockey tournament, Fisher's most important piece of luggage is his flight bag. This flight bag contains approximately 14 paperback books — one for each day of the journey. Before the plane even takes off from Canada, Fisher is reading a book. He must be short-sighted because, invariably, he holds the book about six inches from the end of his nose.

He is a gourmand who will attack his victuals at the most unlikely hours. On the Team Canada tour of 1972, he and Chris Lang were room-mates. Completely exhausted after the flight from Moscow to Czechoslovakia, they crashed in their bedroom at the Yalta Hotel on their first night in Prague.

Lang recalls waking in the middle of the night to see Fisher sitting up in bed with a book poised near the end of his nose. As he sat there, reading, his room-mate was also enjoying a nocturnal snack of smoked herring and a huge slab of rich chocolate cake.

Fisher doesn't waste time on in-flight meals. If the airline serves a filet mignon for lunch, he is likely to split his luncheon roll down the middle, insert the filet between the two sections of bread, and consume this meal without taking his eyes away from the book held in his other hand.

Fisher and Alan Eagleson were wildly dissimilar in personality and style, but they worked together very effectively. It was their joint efforts that persuaded the IIHF countries of Europe to participate in those successful Canada Cup tournaments which began in 1976. Although I never had the good fortune to witness Fisher and Eagleson having a one-on-one argument, it must have been quite interesting — something like a grizzly bear being harrassed by a cocky fox terrier.

Doug Fisher's contributions to hockey have been long-lasting. Among other things, he was a visionary who was among the first to espouse the theories of Lloyd Percival, the ignored Canadian genius who wrote the *Hockey Handbook*. Coaches in the National Hockey League paid no attention to Percival, but his theories were embraced rather extensively by Anatoli Tarasov, the architect of successful Soviet hockey. Strangely enough, in his voluminous writings about the game, Tarasov never has bothered to mention any debt to Percival.

Fisher was such an integral component of Hockey Canada, from its very inception, that his colleagues regretted his retirement from the chairmanship in 1977. Fisher explained his departure by saying: "We had accomplished most of the things which I regarded as our objectives. We had achieved open-competition between our professionals and the Europeans. We had persuaded the Europeans to come to our country for the Canada Cup. And, finally, we were beginning to infuse North American hockey with European techniques and European analyses."

The continuously blazing star in the Hockey Canada firmament always has been Alan Eagleson, the extroverted founder of the National Hockey League Players' Association.

In 1969, Eagleson was delegated by Prime Minister Trudeau and John Munro to be the Canadian Government's official negotiator in all matters concerning international hockey competitions. Most importantly, that appointment has been re-confirmed, without equivocation, by every federal government to hold office since 1969.

Alan Eagleson is the most powerful individual in Canadian hockey. Nothing can be done at the professional level without the approval or, at least, the co-operation of the NHL Players' Association. And Eagleson's contract with the Players' Association doesn't expire until 1993.

By 1993, Eagleson will be 60 and, at that stage, a less dynamic man might give consideration to slowing down. However, international hockey without

Eagleson would be like soda-water without whiskey. Alan is one of those men who will be operating in the mainstream of noisy activity until the day before they transport him to Mount Pleasant Cemetery in Toronto.

It is impossible for the average person to be completely indifferent to Eagleson. He is always receiving the full blast of media attention. The majority of people who know him personally regard him with admiration and warm affection. There is another group — most of whom probably never have met him — who have found themselves embarrassed by his public indiscretions. Giving the Soviets the "middle-finger salute" during Game Eight of the 1972 Summit Series is one example.

Intensity is the word which provides some explanation of Eagleson's public split-personality. He is intensely Canadian; he is intensely loyal to his hockey player clients and his friends; he is intensely devoted to his parents and to his wife and children. Even when he plays tennis — which he does regularly to maintain his keen physical edge — he plays with enormous intensity. His opponent may be his best friend, but Eagleson hammers the ball at him as if he were playing at Wimbledon.

When it comes to pounding out a deal for Canada in international hockey, Eagleson has won the respect and co-operation of the Europeans, even while they are awed by his occasional explosive outbursts. In some respects, Eagleson's public deportment typifies the way Canadians perform in the hockey arena: vigorously, combatively and always quick to take offence at any injustice, real or imagined. Unlike his Hockey Canada colleague, Douglas Fisher, Eagleson doesn't practice intellectual subtlety. Eagleson is about as subtle as a punch on the nose. Nevertheless, he and Fisher formed an effective partnership, and Canadian hockey has been extremely fortunate to be served by two such dedicated men.

From the very beginning, it was obvious that Alan Eagleson must play the major role in Hockey Canada. Even before he came into the Hockey Canada fold, the founding fathers had accepted the principle that Canada's hockey prestige couldn't be restored until we were represented in international competition by the professionals of the NHL. And Eagleson was the man who could deliver those professional players.

Eagleson, Harry Sinden, John Ferguson and the NHL professionals provided the on-ice victory in the Summit Series of 1972. Some Hockey Canada egos were bruised when Eagleson and his group ruthlessly grabbed control of the project, ignoring any well-meant advice from Hockey Canada's governors. It was a case in which the ends justified the means. No one would deny that Eagleson and his inner group deserved the credit for the victory. It was Eagleson who held the 35 players together in the frequent crises which arose after they went to Stockholm and Moscow. He provided the emotional leadership for Sinden, Ferguson and the players, and in their moment of triumph, they gave public acknowledgement of their debt to him.

For all the widely disparate public commentary which he has provoked, there is nothing particularly enigmatic about Alan Eagleson. He is, first and foremost, an uncompromising chauvinist whose greatest joy comes from watching Canada win an international hockey championship.

Louis Lefaive, former president of Hockey Canada.
James Lipa

Whenever I think back over the history of Hockey Canada, the faces which come to mind most readily are those of John Munro, Father Bauer, Charles Hay, Douglas Fisher, Alan Eagleson, Louis Lefaive and Christopher Lang.

Lou Lefaive was the quintessential sports-minded civil servant. He had played football and basketball at Ottawa University; he had coached St. Patrick's College in basketball; and he had been a semi-pro fastball pitcher in his hometown of Windsor, Ontario. He was working for Canada Customs when someone told him that the Department of Fitness and Amateur Sports was looking for a director. He wrote the examinations for the job and was the successful applicant.

Lefaive was the man on the spot when John Munro was looking for a senior member of his Health and Welfare staff who could serve as his personal deputy on the newly formed board of Hockey Canada. Lefaive, a man of much charm and affability, was an ideal choice to play the role of go-between for the volatile Cabinet Minister and the board of Hockey Canada.

However, because it was difficult to find senior civil servants with his sporting expertise, Lefaive frequently was transferred from Hockey Canada to perform other top jobs for the ministry. From 1970 to 1973, he served as director of Sport Canada, then he returned to be chairman of Hockey Canada's International Committee for two years. In 1975, he was again seconded by the federal government to be president of the National Sports and Recreation Centre in Ottawa. He was persuaded to become the first full-time president of Hockey Canada in April, 1979, and he remained in that capacity until 1981. He left the position because he wished to continue working in Ottawa and, at that time, the operating office of Hockey Canada and the National Team was being moved to the Calgary Saddledome. Nonetheless, Lefaive remained on the Hockey Canada board for another three years after resigning the presidency.

Today, he is president of the Sports Marketing Council, that he describes as a "dating-service" for national amateur sports associations that are seeking financial sponsorship from Canadian industrial or financial institutions. He won't be content until he persuades Robin Hood Mills (their advertising emblem is a picture of the longbow-toting outlaw of Sherwood Forest) to be the financial sponsors of the Canadian Archery Association.

In the early days, Lou Lefaive and Chris Lang were running-mates. They looked after the nuts-and-bolts of Hockey Canada while higher-profile governors performed the functions of confronting the public and the news media.

Lang, who grew up in Montreal, graduated from the honours course in Business Administration at the University of Western Ontario. He was to become compulsively involved in sports administration. While working for the Mercantile Bank in Winnipeg at the age of 24, he and Jack Hopwood and a group of other local enthusiasts became supporters of Father Bauer's National Team. This same group of volunteers contributed to the success of the 1967 Pan-American Games at Winnipeg.

With his background, Lang was an obvious choice to be the secretary-treasurer of Hockey Canada. He continues to hold that position, almost 20 years after his first appointment.

A private-enterpriser at heart, Chris Lang has always believed that the federal government shouldn't be saddled with the sole responsibility for funding sports enterprises. He believes that these sports programs must also be supported by the Canadian business community. To this end, he set up his own Toronto office, Christopher Lang & Associates, which he describes as an events and sports marketing company.

In two decades, Hockey Canada's centre of operations has been moved frequently — from Toronto to Ottawa, and back again, and finally to the Olympic Saddledome in Calgary. But, essentially, Lang's office in Toronto has continued to be the financial headquarters and the conduit for the federal government's annual infusion of funds.

Lang's personal rapport with Murray Costello, the president of the Canadian Amateur Hockey Association, probably has contributed to the rapprochement between the CAHA and Hockey Canada. Certainly the two organizations have re-established a fairly cordial relationship, which was notably lacking in previous years.

Christopher Lang had the qualifications for success in any form of endeavour. Fortunately, he devoted himself to sports management, and Canadian hockey has been the beneficiary of his service.

Two men who have contributed significantly to the progress of Hockey Canada in recent years have been David King and Sam Pollock.

Pollock, who was the presiding genius of the Montreal Canadiens while they were dominating Stanley Cup competition from 1965 through 1978, came on the Hockey Canada board in 1979 after he left the NHL to devote himself to private business. Since 1982, he has been chairman of the International Committee, advising and assisting in the selection and operation of the teams

Sam Pollock, chairman of Hockey Canada's International Committee. *James Lipa*

which we have sent to the Olympic Games and the annual world tournaments.

David King joined the Hockey Canada organization in 1982, after he had coached Canada to the gold medals in the world junior championships in Minnesota. It was Canada's first victory in six years of international junior competitions.

A graduate of the University of Saskatchewan and a keen student of the techniques and history of hockey, King coached the Billings (Montana) Bighorns to the Western Hockey League championship in 1979. Subsequently, he coached the University of Saskatchewan Huskies for four years. They reached the CIAU finals in the first three seasons, and they won the Canadian intercollegiate championship in 1983.

King's duties have increased enormously since he was hired by Hockey Canada in 1983 and was given the task of preparing the National Team for the 1984 Olympics. With more and more of Hockey Canada's workload being shifted to the Calgary headquarters, King now has become general manager as well as head coach of the National Team. He and his assistant coach, Guy Charron, are fortunate that Ron Robison, a former CAHA administrator in Ottawa, has arrived on the Calgary scene to take over the duties of business manager of Team Canada.

In 1984, Hockey Canada signed King to a new four-year contract, which carries him through the 1988 Winter Olympic Games at Calgary. Hockey Canada would like to keep King, permanently; however, he has been courted warmly by several NHL clubs. Furthermore, if the International Olympic Committee opens up future Olympic tournaments to professionals, Canada's National Team program may become redundant. No final decision will be made until January, 1988.

Overleaf: 1984 Canada Cup goal. *James Lipa*

Game 1

Exchange of gifts at the opening ceremonies in Montreal, September 2, 1972. Brian Pickell

THE GREENING OF TEAM CANADA '72

8

WHEN COACH HARRY SINDEN AND HIS ASSISTANT, JOHN FERGUSON, waited to greet the members of Team Canada in the lobby of Toronto's Sutton Place Hotel on the morning of Sunday, August 13, 1972, their training-camp roster listed 35 names.

The first man to check in was Bobby Clarke, a handsome, blond youngster who resembled an Ivy League college undergraduate. "Today is my twenty-third birthday," mused Clarke as he sat there, awaiting the players who were to be his teammates for the next seven weeks. "If I was back home in Flin Flon, we'd be getting ready for a wiener roast or something. But here I am, waiting in a hotel lobby while they get ready to flood the ice for the opening of the hockey season."

Within the next hour, the other members of the training-camp squad arrived at the hotel, singly or in pairs. They were scheduled to be at Maple Leaf Gardens at noon, to be checked by a three-man medical staff, which would accompany them throughout the eight-game series.

There had been some changes in personnel, even before the training camp opened. When Sinden and Ferguson made the initial selections in mid-summer, they had included Bobby Hull, Gerry Cheevers, Eric Sanderson, J.C. Tremblay, Ed Giacomin, Walter Tkaczuk, Dallas Smith, Jacques LaPerrière and, naturally, Bobby Orr.

Four of those players—Hull, Cheevers, Sanderson and Tremblay—had signed contracts with teams in the newly organized World Hockey Association. Since the internal politics of the situation dictated that Team Canada would be confined to players from the National Hockey League, Hull, Cheevers, Sanderson and Tremblay had been declared ineligible.

Orr arrived in Toronto, but there was no chance that he would see any action against the Soviets. He had undergone a serious knee operation.

For various reasons, four other men on the original list—Giacomin, Smith, LaPerrière and Tkaczuk—hadn't accepted their invitations. Giacomin had undergone an operation recently; LaPerrière wouldn't go because his wife was having a baby; Tkaczuk had committed himself to work at a hockey camp. Those who didn't accept lost something precious; they missed the most gratifying sporting experience of their entire lives.

Guy Lapointe, LaPerrière's younger Montreal teammate, went on the seven-week pilgrimage although his first child would be born while the team was in Stockholm, en route to Moscow. Lapointe didn't fly home until the final game of the series had been played.

The summary exclusion of Bobby Hull prompted widespread outrage. Even Prime Minister Trudeau got into the act, publicly requesting that the NHL and the NHL Players' Association make an exception in the case of Hull, who had jumped from the Chicago Black Hawks to the Winnipeg Jets.

It was a sticky issue. From the very outset, some U.S. club-owners in the NHL had been reluctant to permit their highly paid players to participate in an off-season series in which they might suffer injuries. President Clarence S. Campbell had exhausted all his eloquence in persuading those club-owners to support the Team Canada project. Now, some of those U.S. owners threatened to withdraw their support if Hull—whose defection from the Black Hawks had been a great publicity coup for the upstart rival professional league—was permitted to play against the Soviets.

The clamor died down as the series-opener neared. Although Bobby's presence in the lineup would have been desirable, the public had decided that the team would be strong enough to win without him.

Bobby Clarke. *Brian Pickell*

Game 2

In retrospect, it was sheer madness to expect that, in 19 days, the players could be whipped into the same physical condition as the Soviets. The NHL players had been out of action since the Stanley Cup final in May. In the interim, many of them had done nothing more strenuous than swinging a golf club or a tennis racquet. Back in 1972, very few professional hockey players indulged in off-season dry-land training. The old, casual NHL approach to a season was, "We'll play ourselves into top shape before Christmas."

Over those 19 days from August 14 to September 2, the players trained hard, but they hadn't been given sufficient time. They were going to meet a Soviet National Team which stressed physical conditioning and which had been playing together, fairly regularly, over the past ten months.

The general public didn't worry about any shortage of physical conditioning as the training camp progressed. They and the Canadian news media had brainwashed themselves, to some extent. The prevailing opinion was that, in the past, the Soviets had been able to overpower North American teams of amateurs or retreaded minor league professionals. Our genuine major league professionals were another story.

It should be emphasized that Sinden, Ferguson and the players never at any time subscribed to the theory that the Russians would be pushovers. They respected their opponents. However, even the members of Team Canada were surprised when the Soviets proved to have been magnificently prepared for the showdown.

The shocking disparity in conditioning was displayed, right in the opening game at the Montreal Forum. The Canadians stormed out of the starting gate as if they were going to win in a runaway. They scored two goals in the first six minutes and thirty-two seconds. By the end of the second period, though, the Canadians were skating on rubber legs while the jet-propelled Russians were flying over the ice-surface.

Probably, the best thing that happened to Team Canada '72 was the 14-day break between Game Four in Vancouver and Game Five in Moscow. In those two weeks, the Canadians took the opportunity to improve their physical conditioning. When they reached Moscow, they were becoming stronger and speedier in every game. In fact, over that final week, they were matching their light-footed opponents in every race for a loose puck.

If, instead of having that two-week breather, the teams had travelled immediately from Vancouver to Moscow and resumed the series with only two or three days of rest, it is reasonable to assume that the better-conditioned Soviets would have won.

Harry Sinden asked himself later, in his series diary: "How did the Russians lose when they can skate as well as us; pass as well as us; take a pass as well as us; play a better team against us and out-condition us?"

"Canadian pros definitely are more accustomed to playing in games with more at stake. Just look at the way we won the final three games, games we couldn't afford to lose. They were stronger physically, but we were tougher mentally. Our mental conditioning—the kind of toughness that comes from playing something like the Stanley Cup—is the thing that, in the end, proved to be the difference."

Game 2

Left: Frank Mahovlich races up the ice. *Brian Pickell*

After Peter Mahovlich's goal, the score is 3-1 for Canada. *Brian Pickell*

When the first training-camp practice was held on Monday, August 12, no one had the benefit of Sinden's hindsight. The attitude was, "There's a job to be done—let's get on with it."

With the established stars of the NHL at their disposal, Sinden and Ferguson had selected a group of big-shooting forwards. Their training-camp roster included 14 of the top 24 point-scorers from the previous season in the NHL. With Orr removed from their plans, they opted for defencemen who, essentially, were recognized for their mobility and skating ability, which would be necessary for breaking up the Soviets' free-wheeling offensive tactics in Canada's defensive-zone.

Phil Esposito had scored 66 goals the previous season. Vic Hadfield had scored 50. Yvan Cournoyer had scored 47 goals. Jean Ratelle had scored 46. Rod Gilbert and Frank Mahovlich had each scored 43.

Sinden and Ferguson had excellent credentials for handling this team of All-Stars. On the surface, their impartiality in dealing with players selected from various NHL clubs scarcely could be questioned. Both men—after establishing formidable reputations in the league—had been out of active hockey for more than a year.

Sinden, after coaching Boston to a Stanley Cup triumph in 1970, had retired to join a friend in the home-construction industry near Rochester, New York.

He also had previous experience in international hockey. He had played for the Kitchener-Waterloo Dutchmen, who lost the 1960 Olympic Games championship. More importantly, he had captained the Whitby Dunlops in 1958 when they won the world tournament at Oslo, beating the Russians, 4-2, in the final.

The end of game handshake, a tradition in international hockey. *Brian Pickell*

Harry never had forgotten the thrill of standing on the presentation podium at Oslo while, to the strains of "O Canada," his country's flag was raised in triumph. It was a thrill which he hoped the members of Team Canada would share many times in the month of September, 1972.

John Ferguson had retired as an NHL player in May, 1971, after eight years in which he had become universally respected as the "heart" of the Montreal Canadiens. He had no coaching experience, but he was widely admired for his mental toughness and his obvious intelligence. Immediately after retiring from hockey, he had emerged as a success in the textile industry. Always popular with the news media, Fergy maintained his high profile in print as an exceptionally proficient race track handicapper for the *Montreal Gazette*.

Below: Phil Esposito and Alexander Maltsev. *Brian Pickell* **Opposite: Jean Ratelle attacks the Soviet net.** *Brian Pickell*

Game 3

It is fair to say that when the Team Canada project first was publicized in the summer of 1972, not every player immediately clamored for the opportunity to enlist. Even The Brothers Esposito, Phil and Tony, had some initial misgivings about the project. It transpired that their agent had been dragging his feet until he was assured that there would be some insurance coverage for the brothers, in case they sustained injuries which might curtail their NHL careers.

After the insurance matter had been straightened out, Phil and Tony joined up whole-heartedly. In fact, Phil proved to be the inspirational on-ice leader of the entire team. Not only did he perform amazing feats in the arenas, but his dramatic appearance on television, after Game Four in Vancouver, ignited the blaze of enthusiasm that sent the team to Moscow, convinced that they would triumph, eventually. As for Tony, he proved to be the more successful of Canada's two goalies: giving up only 13 goals in the four games he played.

At the other end of the spectrum were some players who never had expected to be selected. One of those was Gary Bergman, the 33-year-old defenceman from the Detroit Red Wings. Sinden and Ferguson chose Bergman on the basis of character, rather than outstanding hockey ability. Certainly, Bergman more than justified their confidence by playing the greatest hockey of his career. He was the real surprise package on the team.

Then, there was the case of Eddie Johnston, a really nice man, who for years had shared the Boston goaltending chores with Gerry Cheevers. The original Team Canada goaltending selections were Ken Dryden, Tony Esposito, Ed Giacomin and Cheevers. First, Cheevers was disqualified because he jumped to the WHA. Then, Giacomin was forced to withdraw because he had undergone knee surgery. After losing two of their original four, Sinden and Ferguson invited Johnston to come to Toronto.

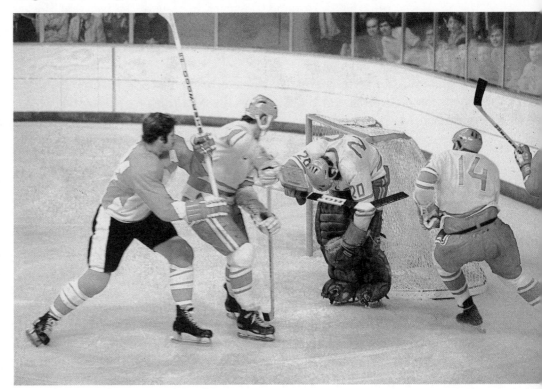

At the training camp, I asked Johnston if he felt slighted because the selectors got around to him only as their fifth choice.

"Listen," Eddie replied earnestly. "I wouldn't have given a damn if they had picked 12 goaltenders ahead of me. Then, if all 12 of those guys had been forced to decline, for some reason or other, Harry and Fergy could have turned to me as their *thirteenth* choice. And, even then, I would have *jumped* at the chance to be part of this team."

Johnston stayed with Team Canada from Day One until they returned to Toronto seven weeks later. He was a true team-man; he was there every day and he never missed a practice. From my admittedly prejudiced viewpoint, I contend that one valid criticism of Sinden's supervision of the enterprise was that he never gave Eddie Johnston the opportunity to play in one of the eight games against the Soviets. Eddie *deserved* the chance to play.

From the outset, the 1972 Summit Series provided a field day for second-guessers, in the public domain as well as in the press boxes. The project had been conceived by Hockey Canada, but in August and September, there was a rather unseemly rush to be front and centre.

Harold Ballard, who a few years later was to proclaim loudly that he'd never permit any Russian performers to appear in his building, made Maple Leaf Gardens available for the 1972 training camp. Ballard also delegated two Maple Leaf employees, trainer Joe Sgro and veteran skate-sharpener Tommy Naylor, to accompany the team through the entire series. Before the training camp ended, the players posed for their first team picture. Ballard smilingly insinuated himself right into the middle of it—sitting in the front row between Sinden and Alan Eagleson.

Privately, the governors and officials of Hockey Canada may have resented being shoved into the background. However, in view of the fact that Hockey Canada was going to profit by approximately $400,000 from the eight-game tournament, they kept their silence as other, more gaudy, performers occupied centre stage.

After all, the series never could have taken place without the full co-operation of two parties: the NHL and the NHL Players' Association. Alan Eagleson, as executive director of the NHLPA, was the man who produced the personnel for Team Canada. Even the NHL club-owners were inclined to be duly deferential where Eagleson was concerned.

When Hockey Canada was formed, three years earlier, Eagleson had declined to accept one of the more prominent seats on the board and, instead, sardonically agreed to be chairman of the public relations committee. Now the chairman of public relations suddenly became boss of the entire shebang.

Sinden and Ferguson were Eagleson-men from the start. In their eyes, he was the one professional in the set-up. They couldn't identify with other members of the Hockey Canada organization who, in their opinion, were merely well-intentioned amateurs.

Sinden's diary for that period indicates that he resented and resisted any attempts by Hockey Canada officials to intrude on the private deliberations of Eagleson, Ferguson, himself and two other members of Eagleson's Toronto staff, Bob Haggert and Mike Cannon. It was Sinden who dubbed this small group "Team Five" as, with each passing day, they tightened their grip on the operation.

This was before the era of investigative journalism in Canada. Consequently, the public—which wouldn't have given a damn, anyhow — was spared the details of any infighting. Nor did the news media bother to pry into the private lives of the hockey players involved. Unquestionably, there were some free spirits in the lineup. On the subsequent trip to Sweden, the Soviet Union and Czechoslovakia, there was a certain amount of freestyle wassailing among a few members of the cast, but none of it was brought to public attention.

In those days, there still existed an unspoken understanding between professional athletes and reporters. The understanding was, "You mind your business, and I'll mind mine." Accordingly, all of the training-camp personnel were treated with nothing but tender, loving care—even those few players who, up to that point, weren't exerting themselves unduly.

One morning, in an intersquad practice game, Vic Hadfield of the Rangers was playing on a forward line with centreman Bobby Clarke. Bobby was one of those players who looked upon even a pre-season practice as being almost as important as the seventh game of a Stanley Cup final. Hadfield, for his part, was a slow starter and, as they say in the profession, "He hadn't been working hard enough to break a sweat."

As Clarke was preparing to take a face-off inside the other team's blueline, Hadfield skated up to him and asked, "Bobby, where do you want me to be on this face-off?"

Clarke glared at him and replied, "I want you to be back on the bench, Vic! That's where I want you to be for this face-off."

Incidentally, from the first day of serious practice, the forward line of Clarke centring the two Toronto players, Paul Henderson and Ron Ellis, appeared to be Sinden's best combination. They were to prove their effectiveness once the series began. Looking back, now, it is surprising to remember that Clarke had been in the NHL for only three years. In the coming season, he won the Hart Trophy, awarded to the league's most valuable player.

In the short period of 19 days, a genuinely high level of team spirit was attained by the Canadians. Sinden had been wondering how 35 professionals, accustomed to playing for money, would respond to the purely emotional challenge of playing for their country. In the 24 hours before going on the ice for the first game in the Montreal Forum, he had his answer. The players were caught up in a surge of patriotism, and they could hardly wait to get out there to meet the Russians.

You may wonder, then, how our best professionals, operating at their emotional peak, could have been beaten, 7-3, by the Soviets in that opening game on September 2, 1972. It is fair to say that the news media had left the Canadian public woefully unprepared to cope with this humiliating loss. I confess to have contributed to the specious proposition that Team Canada '72 would be invincible. Before the series began, I had predicted, in 13 Canadian daily newspapers, that Canada would win seven of the eight games. And I believed it.

Game 4

Above left: Opening ceremonies. Left to right, Goldsworthy, Gilbert, Esposito, Ellis, Park, Stapleton, Bergman. *Brian Pickell* **Far left: Alexander Yakushev coming in for a shot with Viacheslav Anisin.** *Brian Pickell* **Below: Yvan Cournoyer on wing with Frank Mahovlich breaking for the net.** *Brian Pickell* **Middle: Gilbert Perreault.** *Brian Pickell* **Above right: Bobby Clarke.** *Brian Pickell*

Let me explain that, throughout the previous decade, I had become a strong admirer of Soviet hockey. They were playing a style of hockey which, basically, had been played by clever NHL teams, such as the New York Rangers, back in the late 1920s and 1930s. However, I didn't believe that the Soviets were ready to match a team of NHL All-Stars in the early autumn of 1972. In fact, and this was the key to my prediction, I didn't believe that the Soviet team of 1972 was as good as some Russian teams I had watched in earlier tournaments.

For instance, I was one of many Canadian reporters who, only six months earlier, had watched this same Soviet team play in the Winter Olympics at Sapporo, Japan. At Sapporo, the Soviets hadn't frightened anyone. They even appeared to be mediocre in one game when the Swedish National Team, coached by Billy Harris from Toronto, came from behind to tie them, 3-3.

The least impressive feature of the Soviet team at Sapporo had been the performance of their new goaltender, Vladislav Tretiak. Team Canada's two scouts, Bob Davidson and Johnny McLellan, who had gone to Moscow to watch the Russian team in training, came home with a report in which they questioned Tretiak's competence. It transpired that the only game they saw him play was the night before his wedding. Understandably, he was highly nervous.

However, anyone who saw Tretiak play in the Olympics would have agreed with the assessment made by the two Canadian scouts. He was very tentative; he kept his butt well back in his net; he didn't challenge the puck-carriers. Tretiak gave up 13 goals in his five games at Sapporo. By Russian standards, this was unimpressive.

Another point believed to be in Canada's favour was the abrupt dismissal of pioneering Soviet coach, Anatoli Tarasov, immediately after those Olympic Games. Tarasov had been regarded by many as the best coach in the world. And here he was being dumped—to be replaced by Usevolod Bobrov and Boris "Chuckles" Kulagin. Most Canadian observers felt that the wily Tarasov would be irreplaceable.

The real surprise for everyone was Tretiak's performance in September, 1972. There were rumours that, since the Olympics, the Soviets had vastly improved his speed and eye-hand co-ordination by using a swivel-gun to fire pucks at him from every angle. No matter—Tretiak had improved so dramatically that, without question, he was the best Russian performer in the Summit Series.

The public reaction to that 7-3 rout in the opening game at Montreal was nauseating. Some idiots fired off telegrams, insulting the coaches and the players. You would have thought that the Canadian team had deliberately lost the game.

Game Two was played 48 hours later in Maple Leaf Gardens in Toronto. Usually, the spectators in the Gardens are so quiet and polite that members of visiting NHL teams have been known to describe the building as "the world's largest cemetery with lights." However, every Canadian must have been proud of that Toronto crowd on the night of September 4. They screamed their encouragement throughout the full 60 minutes, and the members of Team Canada, reacting to this vocal support, played flawless hockey in defeating the Soviets, 4-1.

Tony Esposito had replaced Dryden for this second game, and the only goal he gave up was a "cheapie" by towering Alexander Yakushev from a net-mouth scramble at 5:53 of the final period. Prior to that, Canada had been leading, 2-0. Only 56 seconds after Yakushev scored, Peter Mahovlich broke away for a short-handed goal, which destroyed the Russians. It was a magnificent solo effort. Mahovlich faked Alexander Ragulin out of his drawers; Ragulin fell to the ice; Peter went around him and blasted a shot past Tretiak.

It is astonishing to look back and realize that the game in Toronto was the only occasion in the series when the Canadians utterly dominated their opponents—outshooting them, 36-21. Never again would they have that type of shooting margin—even in their three victories on Moscow ice. Most remarkably, the Canadians had rebounded to give that magnificent performance only 48 hours after being surprised and humiliated in Montreal.

The first note of any internal dissension was sounded after that Toronto game. Vic Hadfield, disgruntled because his New York Ranger line had been benched after Game One, threatened to quit. Sinden told him that he proposed to give every player on the squad the opportunity to play in at least one game of the series.

Team Canada played very well for 50 minutes in Game Three at Winnipeg on September 6, but in the final ten minutes they were hanging on desperately to preserve a 4-4 tie. It was a case where the beautifully conditioned Russians had a reserve of fresh young legs to throw at their opponents in moments of crisis. The Soviet coaches elected to give some action to their "baby line" of Yuri Lebedev, Aleksandr Bodunov and Viascheslav Anisin, three university students. I don't know what university they had been attending, but they must have been majoring in hockey.

Canada was leading, 4-2, when the Soviet "babies" combined to score two goals in less than four minutes. As had happened in Montreal, the Canadians became very tired in the third period, and the Russians were controlling the play. To give you some idea of the Soviet control, Phil Esposito, who always was the most dangerous forward on the ice for either team throughout the series, didn't have a single shot on the net in that third period.

As the teams moved on to Vancouver, the wolves were beginning to howl again. Even after seeing the Russians playing with such consistent brilliance in three games, the public was grumbling because the very cream of the NHL wasn't burying them. The second-guessers were questioning the manner in which Sinden was changing his lineup. Sinden, for that matter, was beginning to second-guess himself. After that tie in Winnipeg, he wondered aloud why he hadn't stayed with the same lineup that had proved to be so effective in Toronto.

The members of Team Canada were appalled by the greeting they received when they skated onto the ice at Vancouver's Pacific Coliseum for Game Four. Some sections of the crowd began to boo them as an over-anxious Bill Goldsworthy took two well-deserved penalties in the first six minutes, and the adroit Boris Mikhailov promptly tipped in two power-play goals. Although the Canadians served only one more penalty in the remainder of the game, they were unable to capitalize on four Soviet penalties, and the speedy Russians prevailed quite handily, 5-3.

However, the Canadians began to come together as a real team that night in Vancouver. It was Phil Esposito who struck the spark which unified them. Esposito went on national television for an interview immediately after he had changed into his street-clothes. Phil was magnificently angry. I can still see him, standing there with the perspiration on his face, his white shirt-collar unbuttoned, and the knot in his tie pulled down to expose his bare throat.

"I was very disappointed with the people, here," Phil snapped. "I was very disappointed with the people in Winnipeg on Wednesday night. We're playing in this series because we love Canada. And, we're being ridiculed by our fellow-Canadians." He lashed the team's critics, upside-down and backwards. The sincerity of his message couldn't be ignored.

Phil had sounded the rallying call which set the tone for the remainder of the

Above: Paul Henderson in action. *Brian Pickell* **Right: Phil Esposito checks Alexander Yakushev.** *Brian Pickell* **Below right: Bobby Clarke.** *Brian Pickell* **Far right: Paul Henderson in front of the Soviet net.** *Brian Pickell*

series. The public may have been nonplussed by Esposito's fiery eloquence, but he hit the heart of every member of the squad. That impromptu television speech in Vancouver and a couple of incidents which would occur in Stockholm ten days later, bonded the players into a solid group who realized that they must be the masters of their own fate. By the time they left Stockholm for Moscow, they felt that only themselves, the hockey players, could pull it off. For the players, the issue had become "It's us against the world."

The stopover in Stockholm — to play two exhibition games against the Swedish National Team before proceeding to Moscow — became a public-relations disaster. There was nothing wrong in the concept: the stopover would give the members of Team Canada the opportunity to play on a much-larger European ice-surface and, also, it would give them an opportunity to become accustomed to European officiating.

Game 5

The players were duly impressed by their first glimpse of the ice-surface in the Johannesov Arena. "Migawd," said little Pat Stapleton of the Chicago Black Hawks. "It looks like Lake Erie — with a roof over it."

Canadian reporters, who had bitter memories of previous trips to Stockholm with other touring Canadian teams, attempted to warn the NHL players about the type of savagely negative treatment they were likely to receive from the Stockholm press. The warnings went unheeded, and Team Canada walked right into a trap. The Swedish Nationals were ready to bait the Canadians into taking unnecessary penalties. And the tourists obliged. The first game, on a Saturday night, degenerated into an ugly brawl after Ulf Sterner, a Swede who had played briefly in the NHL, speared Wayne Cashman in the mouth and split Cashman's tongue to a depth of two inches.

The Sunday night game was even more depressing. Meanwhile, the Stockholm Sunday papers exploited all the unpleasantness of the previous night. They carried front-page pictures of Swedish players bleeding from wounds, which had been inflicted by the "North American savages." When Team Canada continued to take stupid retaliation penalties in the second game, even the Canadian news media dumped on Team Canada.

That signalled the end of some beautiful friendships. By Monday afternoon, Eagleson, Sinden and the players were receiving transatlantic telephone calls from back home. The callers reported that the news media were hammering the players for their rough-housing tactics in the two exhibition games.

The players felt betrayed — even their own press appeared to have turned against them! They felt that, back home, no one really cared. And now their media corps had deserted them. From that moment onwards, the players felt that they were one small group fighting against the entire world, and the experience moulded them tightly into a self-sufficient unit.

The morale of the players was high the next night when we arrived in Moscow. The wives of the players and team officials had arrived before us with the 2,700 North American hockey fans. The lobby of the Intourist Hotel was jammed by these tourists who gave the team a rousing welcome. The enthusiasm of the North American fans was contagious, and it proved to be inspirational for the team in the remaining four matches.

At this juncture, Team Canada lost four players. Vic Hadfield, upset by the fact that Sinden had failed to include his name in the official lineup for Game Five, said that he wanted to go home to Canada. Eagleson obliged by making arrangements to get him out of Moscow on the first available plane. Immediately thereafter, three younger players — Jocelyn Guevremont of the Vancouver Canucks and Gilbert Perreault and Richard Martin of the Buffalo Sabres — approached Eagleson and asked to be sent home. None of the three had been getting much playing time against the Soviets.

The defections merely stiffened the resolve of those players who stayed with the ship. And the young men who went home lost the opportunity to share what might have been the most glorious winning experiences of their lives.

I had predicted that Canada would win seven out of eight games in the series. Even after the calamity of Game Four in Vancouver, I predicted in our newspapers that Canada would sweep every match in Moscow. I believed that, after that two-week layoff, Canada would chase the Russians out of the Luzhniki Arena.

The loss in Game Five was something that I never could explain adequately to myself or to the readers in Canada. It was utterly inexplicable. It was the only time in the series that the Soviets were able to beat Tony Esposito.

The Canadians were leading, 3-0, at the beginning of the third period, and they appeared to have the situation under complete control. Even when Yuri Blinov scored at 3:34 of the final period, Paul Henderson scored his second of the night at 4:56 to restore Canada's three-goal lead.

Then the roof fell in. It was unbelievable. Team Canada went into a three-minute trance. In those three minutes, the Russians scored three times to tie the game, 4-4. At 14:46, Vladimir Vikulov flipped home the winner. The one gratifying aspect of the performance was the fact that the 2,700 Canadian rooters in the building never surrendered. At the game's conclusion, they gave the Canadian team a sincere ovation, which must have restored the spirits of the players, who had been bewildered by the shock of the Soviet third-period comeback.

I can say, in all honesty, that it was the only occasion in the series when my confidence wavered, momentarily. As I left the Canadian dressing room after the game, to trudge upstairs to the press room, I accosted John Ferguson and asked him earnestly, "Will we beat these guys?"

John replied grimly, "Don't worry. We'll beat them!" I rushed upstairs and I hammered out a column in which I predicted that, without doubt, Canada would sweep the next three games. I don't know if, by that time, anyone back in Canada was prepared to believe a single word I wrote.

Game Six was a gasser! It was the first of those three successive games in which Paul Henderson scored the winning goal. Also, it was the only time in his career that Ken Dryden, while winning, held a Soviet team to less than five goals. But most importantly, Team Canada won, 3-2, while overcoming the horrible officiating of Josef Kompalla and Franz Baader, the West Germans who had permitted those two exhibition games in Stockholm to get completely out of control.

The penalties which the West Germans imposed would have been laughable if they hadn't been so important. As the game was winding down, Canada had been assessed 29 minutes in penalties, and the Soviets had been logged for only 4 minutes. Then, with only 141 seconds left in the game, Kompalla gave a holding penalty to Ronnie Ellis. Ellis, of all people! Ellis had received a total of only 17 minutes in the entire previous NHL season of 78 games.

Nothing could beat Team Canada at that point — not the officiating or the continuing brilliance of the Soviets, who never gave up until the final 34 seconds of the last game.

Game Seven fell into the pattern that was being established on Moscow ice. The Canadians were not to be denied, although, as usual, they took the major share of the penalties. Phil Esposito's two first-period goals were matched by the Soviets, and when Rod Gilbert scored early in the third period, Alexander Yakushev tied it, again, on a power play. Bergman and Mikhailov got into a fight at 16:26 of the final period, and, while they were off, Paul Henderson won it with the prettiest of the seven goals he scored in the series.

There was a face-off in the Canadian zone. Just before play began, Bobby Clarke motioned to his defencemen, indicating that he wanted Guy Lapointe to move slightly to the left, behind the circle.

Then, for approximately the two hundredth time since the team broke training camp, Clarke won another face-off. He slipped the puck back to Lapointe. Young Guy cleared the puck behind the Canadian net to Serge Savard. As this was happening, Henderson, under a full head of steam, was roaring towards centre ice.

Savard hit Henderson with a long, perfectly timed pass, just before Paul sped over the centre redline. At full throttle, Henderson shoved the puck between a lone defenceman's skates. The puck slid through and, without breaking stride, Paul was on it. Still travelling at top speed, he fired a shot which went under Tretiak's left armpit and into the net. Tretiak looked shocked. I believe that, at that point, he was ready for the *coup de grâce* which Henderson delivered in the final game, two nights later.

That third-period fight between Bergman and Mikhailov was unusual in a series that saw little or no real fisticuffing. There was no glass on the boards behind the nets in Luzhniki in those days; only wire mesh, which recoiled slightly when pressure was applied to it. One of the Soviet players, Yakushev, had perfected the art of shooting at the wire screen and positioning himself perfectly to shoot the puck, again, when it rebounded from the screen. He scored one goal against the Canadians on that type of play.

Game 6

Opposite: Ron Ellis threads the puck through a Soviet player's legs to Phil Esposito. *Brian Pickell* **Above: Peter Mahovlich.** *Brian Pickell*

Anyhow, Bergman pinned Mikhailov against the mesh behind the Canadian net. As they struggled, Bergman felt pain in his legs, and he realized that Mikhailov was kicking him. The points of Mikhailov's skates were cutting holes in Bergman's stockings and shin-pads. So, Gary began to pound Mikhailov with both fists. As the punches landed, the Russian's head was bounced back and forth from the loose wire mesh, as if his helmeted noggin was a punching-bag.

For the only time in the series, both benches emptied as all the players in uniform converged on the battling pair behind the Canadian net. To use an old cliché, "cooler heads prevailed," and Bergman and Mikhailov went to their respective penalty boxes. For the life of me, I can't think who the "cooler heads" may have been, because the two European referees for each game seldom appeared to have any situation under control.

For the Moscow populace, there was the chill of imminent defeat in the air that night. About the end of the second period, the snow began to fall on Moscow. When we came out of the Luzhniki Arena approximately an hour and a half later, our shoes left footprints in a half-inch layer of white stuff on the pavement. I don't know why I should have felt surprise, although the date was only September 26. After all, this was Moscow — not Miami, Florida.

What can I tell you, that you don't know already, about Game Eight? Fifteen years later, my few remaining hairs still stand up straight on my head when I remember the excitement. It was worth a lifetime of waiting.

**Returning from the Soviet
net after a Game Six goal.**
Brian Pickell

A happy Canadian fan in Moscow! *Brian Pickell*

MOSCOW, A SEPTEMBER REVISITED

YOU DON'T HEAR THE CHIRPING OF BIRDS IN DOWNTOWN MOSCOW. The birds are somewhere in the city, but they don't come downtown. Probably, they stay away because they fear that they might be arrested for littering the pavement.

In their compulsive dedication to civic cleanliness, the Soviets prohibit littering on their streets. The gendarmes are always on the alert for potential offenders. Foreigners visiting Moscow for the first time have difficulty in distinguishing fact from fiction, but it is rumoured that a litterer can be fined heavily, or jailed, or both. In any event, the uniformed militiamen, patrolling slowly with their hands clasped behind their greatcoats, are ready to reprimand sternly any visitor who has the temerity to drop a gum-wrapper on the city pavement.

The Soviets' devotion to civic cleanliness is admirable; however, it can provide temporary embarrassment for North Americans, who are accustomed to considerably more slovenly public deportment in our own cities. An innocent victim of the Muscovite fetish for cleanliness, when Team Canada and 2,700 supporters invaded the Soviet capital in September, 1972, was Jim Proudfoot, of the *Toronto Star*.

After his first night of sleep at the Intourist Hotel, upon arriving from Stockholm, Proudfoot breakfasted and then, in the spirit of international amity, he sauntered over to Red Square to pay a visit to Lenin's Tomb.

Proudfoot joined the long line of pilgrims who were waiting, silently, for their opportunity to pay their respects at the tomb within the Kremlin walls. Proudfoot, an inveterate consumer of House of Lords Panetelas, was puffing on one of his favourite smokes as he sidled into the ranks of the mourners.

A uniformed militiaman — one of half-a-dozen who were overseeing the daily pilgrimage to the bier — approached Proudfoot. Waving his hands, he made it abundantly clear that smoking while lined up to visit the tomb was strictly forbidden. With a regretful sigh, Proudfoot removed the cigar from his mouth; he dropped it onto the sidewalk and, with his heel, he ground it into the pavement. The militiaman promptly expressed horror. Gesticulating furiously, he indicated that Proudfoot was risking incarceration by leaving a cigar butt on the sidewalk.

Proudfoot doesn't function at full speed early in the morning. He picked up the butt; he looked around; and he couldn't discern any garbage cans. Temporarily baffled, he dropped the cigar butt into the lefthand pocket of his raincoat.

161

A few minutes later, there was consternation in the ranks of the pilgrims. Proudfoot, apparently, hadn't extinguished the cigar, completely, when he ground it underfoot. Now, smoke was billowing from his raincoat pocket.

Proudfoot, blushing furiously, resisted the impulse to deliver an impromptu speech in which he would deny that he was making a political gesture by attempting self-immolation at Lenin's Tomb. Instead, completely fed-up, he carried the cigar butt in one hand and stomped all the way back to his room at the Intourist Hotel where he flushed it down the toilet.

Proudfoot's experience wasn't typical of the adventures of the other North Americans who were visiting the Soviet Union for the first time in that autumn of 1972. Although the constant presence of uniformed militiamen or police was inclined to be inhibiting for the tourists, few visitors ran afoul of the law. A notable exception was the Montreal Boogie-Woogie Bugle Boy who, despite frequent warnings, persisted in blasting away on his trumpet in the Dollar Bar of a downtown hotel. He was lugged off to jail, but he was permitted to leave the Soviet Union when he was released into the custody of a Canadian Embassy official who escorted him to the first-available Montreal-bound aircraft.

There was a certain amount of paranoia, particularly among members of Team Canada. They had been warned that the Soviets might "bug" their hotel rooms, presumably to eavesdrop on any Canadian hockey secrets being discussed in the bedrooms. As for the rest of us, the idea of anyone wishing to listen to the bedside gossip of Canadian tourists was just too ridiculous for contemplation.

Nevertheless, "bugging" stories circulated. The most colourful of these concerned two Team Canada roommates. As soon as they had closed the door behind them, they began to tear the room apart, searching for a "bug." Eventually, they pulled the carpet from the floor and there, sure enough, they found a circular metal plate in the floor.

The metal plate was held in place by four screws, the heads of which were accessible. Working with Canadian 25-cent pieces, the two hockey players began to remove the screws from the metal plate. As the last of the four screws was removed, they heard a distant crash and the tinkling of broken glass. They had unscrewed the overhead lighting fixture in the bedroom directly beneath them.

The story, which was circulated widely in Moscow at the time, has become a part of Canada's hockey folklore. Unfortunately, it lacks confirmation. John Ferguson says that one of the players in question was Frank Mahovlich who, admittedly, was slightly paranoid where the Soviets were concerned. However, Mahovlich denies involvement.

Another source contends that the roommates were Phil Esposito and Wayne Cashman. They, too, deny it. Even if the story isn't corroborated, anyone who visited Moscow in September, 1972, will tell you solemnly that it *could* have happened.

I must be careful how I phrase this, because I am aware that these words may be resented by hypersensitive Winnipeggers. The first time I looked out over Moscow from my twelfth-storey room in the Intourist Hotel, I *liked* the place. Something about it reminded me of Winnipeg, the city of my birth.

Moscow in September reminded me of Winnipeg in April. Viewed from a window of the old Royal Alexandra Hotel, downtown Winnipeg in April had the bruised but indomitable appearance of a veteran prize-fighter who has arisen courageously from a knockdown and who is ready to belt the whey out of his opponent. The cruelly cold Winnipeg winters leave their scars on the buildings of downtown.

Because Moscow reminded me of Winnipeg, I was prepared to enjoy the city, and I wasn't disappointed.

The Soviet tourism agency, Intourist, performed a yeoman chore in coping with and providing amenities for those 2,700 North American invaders. They did their best to provide North American-type food in the hotels. Most of us found the food — particularly the soups and Chicken Kiev — first-class. After hockey games, the ballet, the opera or other escorted outings, a late supper was provided in the hotel dining room. In 1972, there was no shortage of caviar. Huge bowls of it, along with the obligatory black bread, were waiting on the tables for those late suppers. Champagne from the Soviet republic of Georgia could be purchased very inexpensively in Canadian or U.S. dollars.

When the tourists disembarked from their planes at Moscow Airport, they were assigned, in groups, to the bus which would be their conveyance throughout the duration of their visit. For instance, one group would be assigned to a bus, which was clearly distinguished by large window-signs with a picture of a deer's head and the numeral 6. This meant that your particular group was identified as "Deer Six." And every trip you made around Moscow in the next eight days would be made in "Deer Six." A fluently bilingual interpreter was assigned to each bus for the duration of the visit.

The interpreter in charge of the media bus in 1972 was a stocky, handsome lady named Raisa. The bus was identified by a picture of a two-headed donkey, one head facing forward and the other facing backward. Raisa described this bus symbol as "Push-Pull." It was known as "Push-Pull" throughout the length of our stay, but we suspected that it must have been a Russian with a subtle sense of humour who had decreed that the symbol for the Canadian media bus would be a two-headed ass.

Raisa was a cultured lady, in early middle-age, and it soon became apparent that, in addition to being exceptionally knowledgeable about international affairs, she was a person of considerable importance in the Soviet pecking order.

On the night of Game Six (the second game in Moscow), our Push-Pull bus took us from the Intourist Hotel to the large athletic grounds which included the Luzhniki Arena. For the trip from the hotel, Raisa, as usual, was occupying the jump-seat next to the driver.

When we arrived at the gates of the athletic complex, our progress was halted by the militia. Raisa barked an order at the driver, who promptly opened the bus door for her. She descended from the bus in all her majesty. None of us knew what she was saying to the unfortunate leader of the militia. However, with a few words, she destroyed him utterly. Raisa climbed back aboard the bus. She barked a command to the driver. We took off again and half a dozen

militiamen, travelling at a dog-trot, escorted us through the gate and right up to a special parking spot, about 20 feet from the press door to the arena. A Quebec City reporter sitting next to me in the bus, nodded in the direction of Raisa and murmured admiringly, "*très formidable*."

The Soviets had arranged an entertainment schedule which left the North American hockey tourists with little time to get into trouble. Some of the Canadians broke away for overnight trips to Leningrad and Kiev, but those jaunts were also overseen by Intourist guides. On non-hockey nights in Moscow, supervised trips to the ballet, the opera, the Moscow circus and a night-club were scheduled. Those who were looking for unsupervised entertainment found plenty of companionship in the Dollar Bars of the Intourist or the other major hotels. The bars were so-named because they accepted only North American currency.

The famous Bolshoi Theatre was being renovated in 1972. As a result, the regular performances of the Bolshoi Opera and the Bolshoi Ballet were being staged in a magnificent new concert hall which had been constructed within the walls of the Kremlin. From the entrance hall of this building, ticket-holders were transported by long escalators to another foyer, about 50 feet above ground-floor level.

Those must be the speediest escalators in the world. They are so speedy that passengers, on reaching the second-level, are propelled off the treadmill like airline luggage being disgorged from an airport conveyor-belt. Canadians, unaccustomed to such rapid transportation, had a tendency to stand around, admiring their opulent surroundings when they reached the second level. Fortunately, no one was injured seriously, but there were many bruised shins when the passengers jostled one another for space at the top of the escalators.

On that second-level of the huge building, tables were laden with food and drink. Apparently, Muscovites like to have a snack before a performance and another snack at the intermission. When you emerge after the performance has been completed, though, all the tables have disappeared from the foyer. The staples at public entertainment centres appeared to be ice cream and vodka. The Soviets are very big on ice cream, which, invariably, is excellent.

The Muscovites displayed considerable tolerance and patience in coping with the Canadian visitation of September, 1972. The hotel staffs were courteous and helpful. The taxi-drivers, although few spoke any English, always "got you there" with the assistance of little written messages provided for you by the young ladies at the tourist-agency desk in the hotel lobby.

On a Sunday afternoon, when some of us, including Coach John Ferguson, wanted to go to the horse races, we didn't entrust ourselves to the care of a taxi driver. We were driven to the Moscow Hippodrome by Anatoli Seglin, the former Soviet hockey referee. It was a terrible ride, and we were fortunate to survive, uninjured. Anatoli insisted on swivelling his head to talk to passengers in the back seat as we rocketed recklessly through the Moscow Sunday afternoon traffic. That was about the only occasion on which we got away from Raisa's surveillance. She regarded horse racing as time-wasting capitalist depravity.

Phil Esposito in an interview with Dave Hodge. *Brian Pickell*

It's safe to say that 95 percent of the visiting Canadians genuinely enjoyed those evening excursions. Even the trip to the Arabat night club was a pleasant novelty, although I confess that I took much of the pleasure from the running commentary provided by my table-mate, Jim Taylor of Vancouver. When a female gymnast, exhibited tremendous strength by extending herself at a 90-degree angle from a rope hanging from the ceiling, Taylor muttered, "I'll bet that her *real* name is Fred."

The opera, *Boris Godonuv*, was magnificent entertainment for music lovers; however the slobs among us, including most of the media, became a bit restive before the performance was concluded. Raisa took the media grouches to see *Swan Lake*, performed by the Bolshoi Ballet. Even those of us who don't know a damn thing about ballet sat there for the entire evening, absolutely dazzled by the production. The story-line of *Swan Lake* doesn't need to be explained to anyone. You can understand it perfectly. There are two hours of contention between the White Swans and the Black Swans. The White Swans finally win — in overtime!

Most of the Canadians who went to Moscow in 1972 took along a rudimentary wardrobe. The ladies stretched the capacity of their suitcases by including at least a cocktail dress for evening entertainment excursions or for the prescribed afternoon visit to the Canadian Embassy. Ambassador Robert Ford and his staff divided the 2,700 visitors into groups, and every one of them received an invitation to the Embassy.

Knowing in advance that they had been booked to see the opera and the ballet and to visit a night club, most of the men took along one business suit. However, there were some who, throughout their stay in Moscow, insisted upon being seen clad principally in that great Canadian habiliment — the hockey-crested windbreaker.

There are, of course, the notable exceptions to the general rule.

On the evening when Raisa was marshalling the media wretches in the lobby of the Intourist, prior to going to see the Bolshoi Ballet, an elevator door opened and an utterly splendid figure emerged. Herbert Capozzi, the former general manager of the B.C. Lions football club, always has been a bit of a ham, and on this occasion he out-did himself. Capozzi emerged from the elevator clad in full tails, with white tie and waistcoat. He was wearing a gleaming silk top hat; an opera cape draped his shoulders; he carried white gloves; and he was twirling a silver-headed cane. There was a spontaneous burst of applause from the onlookers in the lobby.

For those Canadians who had travelled to the Soviet Union with open minds, Moscow and its citizens provided some pleasant surprises. For example, when the Canadian tourists crowded into Luzhniki for Game Five of the series, they were delighted to hear a superbly bilingual man making all his announcements on the public-address system in English as well as Russian. And, his English had the unmistakable nuances of Canadian English.

The announcer was Carl Watts. Born in the Soviet Union, his parents had taken him to Canada where he was raised in rural Manitoba and Hamilton, Ontario. Later, his father had taken him back to Mocow, and he had worked for the Soviet Union's English-language broadcasting services. Watts also handled the public-address announcements for Team Canada's four games in Moscow in 1974 and, when the world tournament was held in the Soviet capital in 1979, he served additionally as the official interpreter at the press conferences after every game.

Since this book has been, in a sense, a personal narrative, I trust that I may be forgiven for concluding it with three personal recollections of that first visit to Moscow.

When our plane arrived from Stockholm, the hockey players, as was their right, were whisked through immigration and customs without delay. They and their equipment had been loaded aboard their private bus and they were on their way to downtown Moscow while the members of the news media still were attempting to identify their luggage in the jam-packed airport.

An hour later, I emerged from the noisy terminal and was directed to the media bus, which was parked about 100 yards from the airport door. I was wearing a double-breasted private-eye trenchcoat, which I had purchased just before leaving Toronto. I was carrying a portable typewriter in one hand and a briefcase in the other hand.

There I was, an elderly man, stomping along with an exasperated frown on my face. Three uniformed militiamen were standing close to the door of the bus. As I approached, they snapped to attention and the three of them gave me a smart military salute. Obviously, bemused by my age and my official-looking hand luggage, they had mistaken me for some minor Canadian official. Nevertheless, I was charmed by the greeting and my media colleagues, peering from the windows of the bus, were raucously amused by the military reception I had received.

The following morning, I emerged from the hotel, looking for some place where I could get a shoeshine. Less than 100 yards up Gorki Street I found a

Overleaf: Canadian fans in Toronto's Nathan Phillips Square greet Team Canada on its return from Moscow.
Brian Pickell

sidewalk kiosk. It was a very small kiosk, occupied by a very small man wearing a leather peaked cap. Peering in, I could see that there was an elevated seat and two pedestals on which you could rest your feet. The little man ushered me into the elevated seat.

On a shelf, there was a portable radio from which emanated balalaika music. I listened to the music idly while the little man gave me a very good shine. As I descended from the seat, I was groping in my trouser pocket for some Soviet coins. The little man frowned, waved his hands and said *"nyet."* Then, we shook hands gravely, he doffed his cap, and he sent me on my way.

Finally, there was the night of Game Eight in the Luzhniki Ice Palace. After the post-game press conference, I was among the last to leave. I picked up my notebook and my portable typewriter and, emotionally drained, I began a slow walk to the parking lot where a Moscow-based American correspondent was waiting to give me a ride to the office of United Press International.

The lights in the corridors had been dimmed and the big arena was strangely silent. In the corridor, about 50 feet from the press room, a stout middle-aged cleaning lady was mopping the floor.

As I approached her, she looked up and saw the "Canada" button on the left lapel of my trenchcoat. A genuinely friendly smile crinkled her broad face. She cried out, "Ah — Canada," as she threw her arms around me, clasped me to her ample bosom and gave me a great big kiss. It was quite the nicest thing that happened to me on my first trip to Moscow.

In the years since then, I've been musing on the fact that my first sight of downtown Moscow, in daylight, reminded me of Winnipeg. Did I hit on something there? When we lived on Donald Street, my mother had a cleaning-lady, named Lena, who came from Galicia in Russia. When I limped home from the Assiniboine River rink, on frozen feet, Lena would clasp me to her breast and comfort me until my pain and my sobs subsided. I still remember that Lena, who usually had been doing our family laundry, smelled beautifully of soapsuds. I'd like to go back to Luzhniki and find that Moscow cleaning-lady who gave me the great big kiss in 1972. I wonder if she could have been my Lena's granddaughter?

Did I enjoy Moscow? Would I go back, again?

The question already has been answered. I returned to Moscow with Team Canada (the World Hockey Association version) in 1974. And, I made a third trip to the Soviet capital in April, 1979, for a world tournament in which Canada was represented by a group of players whose teams had been eliminated from the first round of the Stanley Cup playoffs.

Yes, and I'd be prepared to go again if Hockey Canada assembled another NHL All-Star Team for a one-on-one series with the Soviets. Even if the building was empty at the time, I'd like to go into the Luzhniki and attempt to find the seat that I occupied when Paul Henderson scored that winning goal in 1972. The building might be empty, but, in my memory, I'd be hearing again Our Crowd triumphantly bellowing the words of "O Canada," and the years would be swept away by an invisible hand.

INDEX